Thoughts

Herbert Windolf

**Publications by Herbert Windolf,
As Translator of Karl May**

Published by Washington State University Press:
The Oil Prince

Published through BookSurge:
Black Mustang
with Marlies Bugman

Published by Nemsi Books:
The Treasure of Silver Lake
The Ghost of Llano Estacado
The Son of the Bear Hunter
Imaginary Journeys I
Imaginary Journeys II
Imaginary Journeys III
Thoughts of Heaven
Winnetou IV
Pacific Shores
The Inca's Legacy
The Scout
Deadly Dust
The Mahdi I

Published through CreateSpace:
The Mahdi II
The Mahdi III
One More Day . . .
As Translator of Autobiography of Isabell Steiner

As Author of Poetic Prose:
Observations and Reflections
Pondering What Is
Otherwise
Musings
Contemplations
Thoughts

Private Printing:
Biography – Bridges Across Times and Continents

Published by Verlag für Tiefenpsychologie und Anthropologie:
Brücken über Zeiten und Kontinente,
Biography – with Dorothea Rutkowsky

Planetary Studies Foundation Quarterly
Travelogues:
A Hike in Provence
A Safari Through Namibia
Alaska, the Last Terrestrial Frontier of the US
Galápagos
Excursions in Saxony's Switzerland
Monumental Sights,
in Grand Staircase/Escalante, Utah, and Northernmost Arizona
Journey to Sumatra
Zambezi
Moroccan Impressions
The Lure of Africa

Planetary Studies Foundation Quarterly
Science Articles:
Snowball Earth
Wondrous Water
The Probability for Intelligent Life in the Universe
Tsunami
Pragmatism
Forty Billion Potentially Habitable Planets,
A Rebuttal

Annemarie Schnitt - Willkommen Website
Translations of Poems and Stories

Unpublished – for Private Use
Autobiography
Translations:
Heinrich Himmler, by Franz Wegener
Ukraine Letters, by Hans Windolf
Germany's Final Months of WWII, Diary of Hans Windolf
The Forgotten Generation, by Sabine Bode
War's Grandchildren, by Sabine Bode
Genesis, by Dorothea Rutkowsky

Courses facilitated:
From the Spice Trade to Globalization
Cataclysms and Extinctions
The Likely Futility of SETI Programs
The Cambrian Explosion
Human Evolution and Migration
The American National Mind vis-à-vis the Rest of the World

Addendum
A Collection of Haiku Verses

Content   Page

Content	Page

Content	Page

Content	Page

Content	Page

Content   Page

In Closing

Introduction

This introduction will be short with just a few thoughts gleaned from other people.

Jean-Baptiste Poquelin, known by his stage name Molière, a great comedian, is said to have claimed: *"All which is not prose is verse; and all which is not verse is prose."*
Well, maybe he was mistaken after all, for I claim three hundred fifty years later that what I call my "Poetic Prose" is simultaneously verse and prose, using meter and rhyme, but is not poetry as customarily written.

As claimed in my Introduction to Musings, I feel a kinship with this other Frenchman, Michel de Montaigne, the inventor of the essay (*essai* in French), who, in short tracts four hundred years ago, wrote factually about himself, his world, and life in general. I do the same in my Poetic Prose, not with his sophistication, though more briefly.

In his book "*Why*", the author, Mario Livio, names Montaigne, who urged his readers to probe the mystery of everyday things.
I cannot help doing something similar. Sometimes I write about mundane subjects, often elaborating on items of interest to me which is hoped will be of interest to others. At times I can even be funny.
But what Livio explores is the trait of Curiosity, the Stimulus of the New, in its various manifestations in humans. While he does not much attribute Curiosity to the other creatures of our world, it, in a less sophisticated

form, exists across the entire spectrum of life. I only have to think of my cat Rikki with her need to explore the new.

Certainly Curiosity is not found equally among individuals, animal or human. Some are more timid, others more dull, and some more curious.

Livio names four types of curiosity: *Perceptional curiosity*, which arises from novel experience, fading over time. *Diversive curiosity being the restless desire for novel stimulation to avoid boredom,* such as *the constant checking for new text messages.* Then there is *Specific curiosity, the desire for a particular piece of information.*

And lastly, *Epistemic curiosity, the veritable desire for knowledge, Kant's "Appetite for Knowledge."*

Without wanting to delve too deeply into this subject matter, I return to the secondary purpose of writing my Poetic Prose, the primary one being my desire to explore the one or the other subject for my own benefit, or to document past experiences to illuminate where I have come from or how my eyes see the world.

And this has brought me full circle to my soulmate, Michel de Montaigne, if I may be so presumptuous. Oftentimes I like to "rattle the chains" of one or the other of my sensitive readers to explore more deeply that which I only touch upon.

Last not least my thanks go again to my editors and proofreaders, Lynn Chesson and Zene Krogh, who keep me out of trouble, not being a native speaker of English, or rather the American language.

Finally, let me mention here that I have used, with her permission, several of my wife Ute's photos as covers for my publications. The cover image of my last publication, *Thoughts*, dates from her black-and-white period. It is her favorite one, milkweed, food and reproductive plant for the Monarch and Painted Lady butterflies, its feathery seeds being carried away by the wind, just as my thoughts are or will be.

Herbert Windolf   Prescott, AZ

Thoughts

Blown in the wind,
like milkweed seed pods,
Monarch butterfly food,
ephemeral, come today,
defined, refined, gone in a spin.

It is the Vague and Elusive.
Meet it and you will not see its head.
Follow it and you will not see its back.
Lao Tzu

To Weep

The shedding of tears so human is,
an expression of grief, of sadness, of joy.
Alone we are in the mammal world,
where emotion powers the shedding of tears.
This isn't to say that our animal kin
cannot wail or howl in discomfort and pain.
Yet here's a difference between them and us:
We are equipped with the bigger brain
– for better or worse –
to, at times, see our stronger emotions
peacefully reign.

Man is the only animal that blushes. Or needs to.
Mark Twain

Follies

No, not the Folies Bergère
in Paris of old,
you may be thinking of,
which, in nineteen-sixty,
I saw when the dancers were still enrolled.
No, "folie" in French means "crazy, mad."
This is what humans are at root,
when all is said.

If you wish to be loved, show more of your faults
than your virtues.
Edward George Bulwer-Lytton

3

Animals

Of all the animals that abound in this world,
we are just another species among the lot,
ruled by instincts and emotions,
colloquially called – by the gut,
mostly that is, more often than not.
Sometimes I wish we'd truly succeed,
to metamorphose into another breed.

I am the only person in the world
I should like to know thoroughly.
Oscar Wilde

Metamorphosis

Oh do I ever wish we humans
could go through a metamorphosis,
changing from our contradictions aplenty
into a form, taking flight, becoming cognoscente.
But, no, not to be just at home in the world of arts,
of specific knowledge, but to know it All.
To make ratio our intimate home,
powered by emotions encoded in a single genome.
Alas, evolution is slow,
and we may never get there.
Should we, or shouldn't we?
Should we even dare?

What we anticipate seldom occurs;
what we least expect generally happens.
Benjamin Disraeli

Juncture

Am I wrong, am I right
in thinking that we've arrived at a juncture,
where one path may lead to a future bright,
the other to a descent into hell,
just in sight,
or as usual, keep muddling on as we might?
Did we arrive at a minor blip
when it appears our future might take just a
minor dip?
Or is it a juncture where we play with fate,
when we, at least some, know better
which route to take?
Do we truly know what is good for us?
What we should do, what would be a loss?
But, as always, a thorough muddle it is,
a lot of fizz, not subject to analysis.

Cynic: A blackguard who sees things as they are,
not as they should be.
Ambrose Bierce

Depression

Sometimes I feel it coming on,
a chemical reaction on the run.
More often it's caused by life's little ways,
which can bring on a low to last for days.
Then I rise once more to the light,
and the future again looks more shiny and bright.

If you know life, give me your address.
Jules Renard

Scents

Human scenting is not on a par
with dogs and cats and bears by far.
And many folks with their noses untrained,
their sense of smell is poorly maintained.
Passing a woman or a man
the odor they carry wafts past as if fanned.
It's oft a composite of their bodies, their home,
the stuff they put onto them,
and whether they smoke.
Women who often "live" their makeup, their
perfume,
are unaware how they impose their scent
onto others who may not appreciate
being exposed to it,
even if wearers so assume.

Grace imitates modesty,
as politeness imitates kindness.
Joseph Joubert

Tails

Some are short, some bushy,
some long, some are tall.
They help their owners keep balance,
prevent a fall.
Humans, without one,
have no balance at all.

In life, we are all in the gutter.
Some of us just tend to look up at the stars.
Oscar Wilde

Shade

Twice a day I take my cat Rikki
out for rather long walks.
On a harness and leash that is,
which she accepts but against which she also balks.
We amble along the street,
through bushes, under trees,
but cats aren't like dogs
who run with their masters.
Often Rikki rather sits and watches at ease.
She's smart – smarter than some folks –
to always find shade
while I, taller, stand in the sun, I'm afraid.
Adding insult to injury, as I found out at last,
she often comes to rest in the shadow I cast.

I cannot teach anybody anything;
I can only make them think.
Socrates

Brittle

Some people come across brittle as glass,
others are congenial and friendly.
The former tend to put distance between
themselves and the many of us,
those reaching out without fear of loss,
of being hurt or rejected,
or being crossed.

Compliments are often insincere,
but fault-finding is always genuine.
Edgar Watson Howe

11

Denial 1

Fundamentalist people
hold Earth to be just six thousand years old.
They happily fly across country,
use electricity, a fridge, their car, and much more,
all science's offspring, technology, for sure.
Their cell phones are handy,
based on satellite technology
with quantum mechanics at root.
They rely on science day in and day out,
except when it comes to evolution,
geology, paleontology, and dating methods.
Since these contradict their irrational beliefs,
they deny what the real world is about.

Never argue with stupid people, they will drag you down
to their level and then beat you with experience.
(Or is it certainty)
Mark Twain

Reaching Out

Neighbors of mine lost their cat overnight.
Of a heart attack she might have died.
Thirteen years old, beloved she had been,
her owner, a woman,
grieving the loss of her little queen.
I take my Rikkicat out every day,
on a leash, that is,
to prevent her curiosity from running away.
When I saw the lady puttering in front of her home,
my cat and I walked over to bid her the time of day.
It was my intention to give the woman a choice,
to keep grieving or to reach out,
to pet my Rikki,
leaving sadness behind, to rather rejoice.
Alas, I failed in my intent.
She was not able to reach out
for her grief to transcend.

Sometimes even to live is an act of courage.
Lucius Annaeus Seneca

Stimulation

We all need it, young and old,
humans and animals for life to unfold.
Any creature stuck in a routine
will lose brain cells, become a has-been.
A has-been in the joy, the rapture of being,
the hunt for the new,
of reflection, action, loving and seeing.

The greatest virtue of man is perhaps curiosity.
Anatole France

Rock Hopper

No, not the penguins in Antarctica,
but rather this writer a rock hopper was
able to leap from boulder to boulder in years past,
whether across a creek or other traverse.
Alas, these agile days are gone for good.
Nothing remains and nothing lasts.

In matters of grave importance, style,
not sincerity, is the vital thing.
Oscar Wilde

Discipline

Discussing subjects of manifold kind
is a joy to pursue, to explore, to learn,
and, lo, at times something new to find.
But its bane is often the trend to drift
from the subject at hand often all too swift,
and lost is the theme, now getting short shrift.
This problem calls for awareness, discipline,
to beware of the often subtle shift,
which departs from what is essential,
and leaves the discussion adrift.

The education of the will is the object of our existence.
Ralph Waldo Emerson

Flowers

How monochrome would the Earth be without.
But one-hundred-thirty million years ago
we know without doubt,
before the first flowers evolved and fanned out,
the world was much poorer in color,
except for the feathers the dinosaurs showed.
Then arose the family of orchids,
the most prolific of flowering plants,
and never again was color scant.
Today found in meadows and on trees,
once difficult to propagate,
now sold in stores everywhere.
One keeps gracing my home,
lasting weeks at a time,
replaced when its blossoms no longer shine.

All gardeners live in beautiful places
because they make them so.
Joseph Joubert

Scatterbrains

What is the trouble with some folks in this world
who dibble and dabble,
do not hear what's been said,
forget what there is to be done,
who cannot get organized,
and can't find what they've mislaid?
Prone they are, too, to miss a date.
A sworn enemy it is for them to keep time.
Thus they waddle through life
without reason or rhyme.
Behold, though, some are still able to grow
and make their life a successful show.

I was working on the proof of one of my poems all morning,
and took out a comma,
In the afternoon I put it back again.
Oscar Wilde

Denial 2

Oh, you proud creations of man,
New York, Miami, London, Amsterdam,
and the many others at continents' rim.
The globe is warming, there's no doubt.
All points in the direction of this route.
Many of you deny the oceans' rising apace,
but warm water is known to need more space,
and in due course will millions of people displace.
What will you do with the waters rising?
When your denials and short-term minds
come to an end and you must face
the manifestations, the signs,
too late it is then for you to mind?

It is through science that we prove,
but through intuition that we discover.
Jules Henri Poincare

Grebes

They walk the water with power and grace.
Have you ever seen them perform their mating dance?
In unison they move their heads,
sideways, looking left and right,
swiftly, then again each other they face,
all the while walking their beautiful prance.
A supreme enjoyment it is to watch them dance.
Here and there you may have heard some talk,
but it's not only humans who on water can walk.

Beauty is the promise of happiness.
Stendhal

Greed

There's nothing wrong with a smidgen of greed,
to acquire in life what there is to be had.
It propels its pursuers on to provide
for themselves and others a better life.
If it waxes for status, power and riches,
it may still provide work, sustenance,
and decent conditions for those without vision.
But if only pursued for power and wealth,
where's the limit of mental health?
What is there lost in the pursuer's mind,
if he exploits his surroundings,
does not share with his kind?
Today, an impressive array
of people who've made it, give their winnings away.
Thus I finish this verse with a salute to these folks,
with a resounding, admiring hip-hip-hurray!

All art is autobiographical;
the pearl is the oyster's autobiography.
Federico Fellini

Mind

In a superficial way we relate.
As children, most of us,
in certain behaviors are trained.
Schooling continues the process
and whatever else by life's exigencies
is to be learned.
Genes are the basis from which the above arises,
to form a composite of many surprises.
There is a continuum from dull to smart,
from troubled to sane, from considerate to harsh,
from organized to frazzled,
a collection of minds à la carte.
Some of these characteristics keep us together,
while, on the whole, they keep us apart.
It is a wonder we usually get along.
Sometimes I marvel about this work of art.

Every man's work, whether it be literature or music or pictures
or architecture or anything else, is always a portrait of himself.
Samuel Butler

Surreal

How is it that I lately perceive
the world, human actions, as phantasmagorical,
bizarre, grotesque, freakish, unearthly,
a dream-like weave?
Can the world be so surreal,
so silly, so weird?
Are my glimpses, my lucid moments,
to be feared?
Or is it the truth
the way they appear?

In a November '17 interview Salman Rushdie
called the current state of the world,
especially that of the West,
"a disengagement from reality."

Birthday Wish

For my wife's eighty-first birthday
I sent her a card,
wishing her the best
for what is yet to be had.
And following "Happy Birthday to you," I wrote
"May you find what you are looking for,
and may what you aren't looking for, find you."

During times of universal deceit,
telling the truth becomes a revolutionary act.
George Orwell

Crash Landing

It was in nineteen-sixty-six
when I boarded a plane in Chicago
to take me back to my then home,
the Canadian city of Toronto.
Late night it was
when the turboprop Viscount took off,
carrying seventy people aloft.
Scared of flying in these aluminum bins,
I took valium at the time to ease my fears,
and always sat at the emergency exit over the wings.
At last I heard the bumps, getting ready to land,
the landing gears make when they extend.
Once, twice, three times the sound arose,
and I knew this plane now had its woes.
And the captain came on "Ladies and gentlemen,
we have a small problem,
nothing to worry, we'll solve it going along."
He came to the cabin,
shone a light on my side of the wing,
asked the fellow sitting before me,

"Can you see the red pin?"
Yes, he still saw it, which the pilot told
that this gear was still in the aircraft's hold.
We circled Lake Ontario for an hour or more,
dumped plenty of fuel,
meanwhile they foamed the runway
to skid safely home.
Then came the time when we arrow-straight
slid on two wheels and the wing on my side.
Sparks flew aplenty, with the props bending back.
Once having come to the halt, I opened the hatch
and was the first one out in a flash.
Thereafter I decided to bid valium goodbye
and since then fly without,
even held my seat neighbor's hand
when a big DC10 was about to bumpily land.
Yet, I still prefer a four-seater Cessna's flight
flying low over the African countryside,
below seeing giraffes and elephants stride.

Experience without theory is blind,
but theory without experience is mere intellectual play.
Immanuel Kant

Having Class

We live in a time when many a man,
and certainly women, too,
have risen from rather downtrodden ways
to a better than average class.
But they haven't learned – or have they lost? –
the manners and wherewithals to behave.
What I've seen on TV many Russians know,
better than Americans to clink with a glass.
The latter hold them at the bulb, not the stem,
thus the beautiful sound a clinked glass makes,
is utterly wasted by them.
The oft slovenly dress could use an upgrade,
how to properly use cutlery,
and what type of glass goes with what,
could stand some improvement, some etiquette.
I could go on, snob that I am, to list plenty more,
God forbid.

A gentleman is one who never hurts anyone's feelings
unintentionally.
Oscar Wilde

High Tundra

Some years ago near Denali Park
we took a helicopter ride to the surrounding hills
where trees no longer grow as Nature wills.
When our pilot, a young woman, heard
that from Prescott we were,
she exclaimed "I got my license there!"
Up she took us to the bare rolling hills,
where we walked for hours forth and back
across the squishy soggy landscape,
a monotone grey-green its color,
at times broken by a bleached caribou rack.
The scrubby ground cover barely a foot high,
its willow trees miniatures in the climatic chill.
The starkness held beauty,
I remember it still.

Everything has beauty, but not everyone sees it.
Confucius

Albacore

Today I prepared a salad for lunch,
with red pepper, onion, pickle, and tomato,
not to forget salt, pepper, lemon juice and mayo,
and as its base the flesh of tuna.
You were spawned an Albacore
and survived predation to grow.
Then schooled in Pacific tropical waters,
a predator yourself you went with the flow
cruising the deep blue waters below.
Above, other predators cast the nets-of-man,
caught, you saw the light of day.
I think of you, fish!
Even when for me to eat
you ended up in a metal can.

As soon as there is life there is danger.
Ralph Waldo Emerson

From the Heart

It seems to me
that the verses I write
are basically of two different kinds.
One is produced by the reasoning mind,
the other, somewhat from the above athwart,
is usually better,
since it comes from the heart.

He that leaves nothing to chance
will do few things ill,
but he will do very few things.
Halifax

Intuition vs Reason

We have two approaches to deal with the world,
of whatever impinges on our mind.
The primary one is intuitive,
spontaneous, visceral, emotional,
based on experience and belief,
whatever we have assembled in time.
It usually serves us very well,
at other times, when too rigidly held,
it may lead us astray, which isn't swell,
when thoughts come to mind as if rung by a bell.
Political positions, responses to those,
are an example, I propose.
The second, our reason, as far as applied,
requires logic and induction,
being of a slower kind, taking time to decide,
such as multiplying twelve by twenty-five,
comes to mind.
This is why we ought to slow down for a reply,
to whatever it is that comes our way,

31

to give our slower but more rational mind
the time to consider a more appropriate response,
a better try.
Provided our lazy rational brain
won't leave the answers to intuition,
thus all being in vain.

No persons are more frequently wrong,
than those who will not admit they are wrong.
François de La Rochefoucauld

Cadence

Some people won't give a poem
the time of day.
We can't all be the same, but that is okay.
It also depends on the kind of poem,
as it may.
But when folks without affinity to poetry
must read a poem in public,
all too often having no sense
of cadence, meter and tempo,
of rhythm and rhyme,
they mangle its beauty,
never get it to chime.

All bad poetry springs from genuine feeling.
Oscar Wilde

Friend

There is this friend of many years,
of decades even, I know, it is.
His abode is way up in Germany's north.
In the past we visited each other,
now it's only phone calls going back and forth.
We both live alone,
he more so than I,
thus the calls we make,
with nothing deep to dwell on,
are nevertheless, telling us
that we value each other,
that we belong.

Don't walk behind me; I may not lead. Don't walk in front of me;
I may not follow. Just walk beside me and be my friend.
Albert Camus

Exaggeration

At times it is helpful when making a point
to amplify what one wants to convey.
The point's meaning is too easily lost
to many a non-listener, if not most,
which is why it is wise to give it a boost.
The boost gives the point the desired jolt,
exaggeration it is,
but why not be bold?
Tempted I was to rhyme with dolt,
but of poor taste it would be
and cause a revolt.

It is the confession, not the priest, that gives us absolution.
Oscar Wilde

Pooped

I still entertain, and enjoy it, too,
but when all is cleaned up and done,
and I am ready to go to bed,
sorely pooped I am.
My libations are kept to my usual two,
but food's still enticing
which might me undo.
It may be just age,
or whatever is wrong.
But a favorite saying of my father's was
"Intelligence guzzles,
and stupidity crams."

If thought wilt make a man happy,
add not to his riches
but take away from his desires.
Epicurus

Blazing Away

My darnedest I'll try
to keep doing things my way,
interact, procure, and convey,
until something will get me.
But till then,
to the very last day,
I'll give it a good shot,
better to go in a blaze
than to fade away.
Do I wish!

We need to love to be healthy,
and we might get sick when we have
no opportunity to love.
Sigmund Freud

Sanity 1

How many of us are truly sane?
To think and act rationally,
a state of mind so hard to attain.
What is "sound mental health?"
Can it truly be found?
How many or few of us
are really sound,
stable, sensible, prudent and wise?
How many are somewhere "off,"
visible or covert?
I, too, have my idiosyncratic quirks.
To maintain sanity is awareness helpful
by recognition, understanding, insight,
this being true consciousness?
Are some forms of insanity
creativity's consequence?

We think very few people sensible except those
who are of our opinion.
François de La Rochefoucauld

38

Overreach

---

it was, I wanted, and I want it still today.
Reach the other, mind to mind,
at times, when both are so inclined.
To feel the other's deepest thoughts,
to share mine, understand directly,
spared the common verbal onslaught,
which, slow, deals in metaphors, in similes,
trying to describe what's felt,
and struggles with analogies,
words, in which the rational mind dwells.
This overreach can't come to pass,
I know, I know, I'm stuck with molasses,
or brittle, inaccurate verbal glass,
used to describe what is felt, what is.
I know, I know, for I failed in this way,
which is why I wish for this overreach
to miraculously access directness, still, to this day.

You will either step forward into growth
or you will step back into safety.
Abraham Maslow

39

Structure

----

is required to accomplish something,
of whatever nature it be.
I have been an organizer by nature,
one ability given to me.
While I need it myself to get ahead,
I find it stifling when instead
it limits my freedom, and not only mine,
to flexibly address whatever the problem,
but rather a certain pattern confine.
Ah, the freedom to adjust to whatever comes along,
to solve a problem with or without structure,
and then some.

Your theory is crazy, but it's not crazy enough to be true.
Bertolt Brecht

Desktop Display

MacOS Version 10.13.1, Apple just released,
is called High Sierra.
With this new display I'm highly pleased.
I could gaze at this image time and again.
Compliments to its selector, woman or man!
The aspens' fall colors, yellow and red,
are aglow, are so vivid, could I only sit
at the proximal shore of the lake,
looking across where two creeks end their run at its
bank.
But the times where I could sit there
are certainly gone.
It is way too high in the Sierras
for an eighty-one-year-old man,
but who can still admire what Apple has done.
Dark patches of scrub rising
from the valley up slopes.
Trees dapple valley and heights
to where snow stops their daring climb.

Brownish scree covers other declines,
and behind and at left
rise rugged snow-covered mountains,
a backdrop, vitality defined.
But the glow of the aspens
is what gives the image its glorious life.

The creative person is both more primitive and more cultivated,
more destructive, a lot madder and a lot saner,
than the average person.
Frank Barron

If Only

I had the wherewithal,
the wiring of the brain
to understand more of the world,
yet I know, by far not all.
I've read of the Greats of science and art
and long to approach,
just come closer to that which they
comprehended, came from their very being,
from their Heart.
Alas, I am stuck with my mediocre mind.
Unlikely, should I ever be born again,
I may come closer to their very kind.
I must content myself to be
that which I am to set myself free.

All of life is education and everyday is a teacher
and everybody is forever a pupil.
Abraham Maslow

Inkling

I do a number of gymnastic exercises,
or, when I go shopping
keep six or seven items on my mind.
Then, when I'm done
and think I have them all,
there remains this faint inkling
that one is missing.
Come on, "get on the ball!"
My mind is whispering
"You haven't got them all."
This intimation, the memory's call,
then rises to the conscious mind
and, lo and behold,
there, surfacing, comes the missing recall.

He who doesn't lose his wits over certain things
has no wits to lose.
Gotthold Lessing

Birdbath

Commonly called thus,
the name's not quite true.
Birds do bathe in them
but more often they drink.
Trust me, this is what they do.
There is this nice neighbor
with a fancy bath of glass.
The bowl is quite deep,
with its edge hard to grasp.
Thus its purpose is defeated
to drink or to bathe.
The setup is nice,
but "it is for the birds."

When the solution is simple, God is answering.
Albert Einstein

You,

---

the one I love,
but who seeks distance between us.
You, with whom I feel at home, no other comes close.
You, I have need for in my final years,
if only to reminisce about the good things we shared.
You, who have need from the shadows to rise
to leave the world of the Bad behind,
to yet grow and find your very self.
You, like me, learning
to express what we need for a final beginning,
if ever again we are able to meet.
You, to find the strength to forgive, not forget.
You, to find all that you seek,
and more of it yet.
All this before it is too late.

Hope is the last thing that dies in man;
and though it be exceedingly deceitful, it is of its good use to us,
that while we are traveling through life
it conducts us in an easier and more pleasant way to our
journey's end.
François de La Rochefoucauld

Acculturation

It must've been in '84
when I took an independent study
in anthropology,
with my instructor, an Afghan PhD.
A Muslim he was, and we ranged far and wide
challenging each other in good stride,
the most I ever experienced
with any of my professorial guides.
At the end of the course
I invited him, his wife and teenage son,
for a dinner at my home,
requiring a one-way fifty-mile run.
He gladly accepted but asked quite nicely:
"Could I bring my brother
who's visiting from Germany,
there married to his German wife?"
Of course, I said, and it was done.
We didn't serve pork, but beer was okay,

and when I mentioned a German after-dinner-drink,
the German Afghan had given it a try,
thus we men had a round,
nothing kept us at bay.
But the visit was interesting in another way.
The American Afghan sat there in pullover, relaxed,
while the German Afghan, in suit and tie,
sat most formally at the dinner table,
acculturated differently, quite a contrast.

The world is divided into two classes, those who believe the incredible,
and those who do the improbable.
Oscar Wilde

Fear

'T was in the Galapagos, back, a few years
that I experienced genuine fear.
Our group of twelve left our yacht in a motorboat
to skipper to an area where we were to float,
to snorkel, observing the sea life below.
The water was about ten feet deep,
dotted by basaltic, sharp-faced volcanic mounds,
each about four feet high and twelve feet wide.
I snorkeled along, my eyes below,
when I suddenly noticed "I am alone!"
Our boat, the group nowhere to be seen,
I was lost in an open sea, a directionless scene.
The mounds were impossible for a footing to find.
Never a good swimmer
I had to take control of my mind.
Forceful strokes brought the boat into my sight,
to which I now headed to find rest from my plight.

With the fortunate everything is fortunate.
Horace

49

Cat

There, right in front of me,
in the middle of my desk,
blissfully, lies my cat at rest.
Not even a twitch of the tail she makes.
I do not dare leave,
for it's my company she craves.
Might I be able to rise, go fetch my book,
to return in time,
might this get me off the hook?
What all one does
for a creature one loves!

Love is of all passions the strongest,
for it attacks simultaneously the head,
the heart and the senses.
Lao Tzu

To Know

From Socrates to Rumsfeld
we have dealt with "to know."
We know there are "known knows,"
like the sun will keep shining
or how to make beer.
Then there are the "known unknowns"
that an earthquake will strike,
or a volcano will erupt.
We know it will, but unknown its time.
Last there are the "unknown unknowns,"
of things we have not the faintest idea.
When they confront us, out of the blue,
they are certain to cause wonder
and likely fear.

We do not yet trust the unknown power of thoughts.
Ralph Waldo Emerson

Curiosity 1

All creatures are curious,
just think of a cat.
But Man is the most,
propelling him to the top of the pack.
Most varied our curiosity is
reaching from the mundane,
playing the smart-phone game,
to come across something new,
to specifics, like to remember a name.
Last, but not least, is the crowning pursuit
of knowledge per se,
the curiosity impelling us
to learn of what the world is made.
And why are we and animals curious at all?
It is a stimulus, a positive feedback,
providing life with its sprawl.

There is no sin except stupidity.
Oscar Wilde

Alive

Right in front of me on my desk,
lies a small creature,
which cannot find rest.
It moves left and right, down and up,
it is patterned beige, grey and black.
It is but a few inches long,
amazingly, it is quite strong.
I wonder why it moves so much,
what is its drive?
It is fun to observe
being so much alive.
All this when I know in fact,
it is the tail attached to my cat.

We know how to speak many falsehoods
that resemble real things, but we know,
when we will, how to speak true things.
Hesiod

Cursed

I have a sensitive nervous system,
which keeps racing ahead,
when intensely engaged
in a problem to be solved,
a conversation having been held.
Mentation keeps pounding on
late into night or even morn'.
A major dread, it keeps sleep at bay
when the need is so great,
following an intense day.
Aroused, the turmoil cannot be stilled
by neither meditation nor will.

A hero is one who knows how to hang on
one minute longer.
Novalis

Ignoring

There was this friend
of Turkish descent,
together, many years we had spent.
When he was ill we had walked,
and we had talked and talked,
of whatever crossed our minds, never balked.
One day he "confessed" that he had voted "right,"
while I had always thought him to be bright.
Then came the time for his annual trip
to Turkey, his fatherland,
and verily he lost his grip when I told him
"Why travel from one misgoverned country to the
next?"
To which he rudely in public blew his top.
Truly and visibly he was vexed.
I did not respond, didn't make a scene,
from then on just engaged
in the restaurant surroundings' routine.

Ignoring the man, mentally having said
"goodbye,"
I succinctly expressed how he had gone awry.

No one ever became thoroughly bad all at once.
Decimus Junius Juvenal

Curiosity 2

Once more I address curiosity,
the positive feedback mechanism
across all life.
It is a learning mode making creatures more fit,
the most curious creature – humans –
are therefore ahead of all other life,
I must admit.
Whether it will do us good
in the long run,
is something to be found out,
I submit.

The madness of individuals is an exception.
The madness of groups, parties, nations and epochs
is a rule.
Friedrich Nietzsche

Certainty

All our efforts from ages past
have been directed toward making things last,
from religions and nations,
to science and technology,
to compensate for Nature's uncertainty,
so utterly vast.
This got us to where we are today,
yet, perversely, we are prone, again and again,
to lead ourselves astray.
When are we going to learn Nature's law
that there is no certainty?

Sometimes people don't want to hear the truth
because they don't want their illusions destroyed.
Friedrich Nietzsche

Talking About It

I've been chided that some verses of mine
are too morose, addressing death,
giving reason to pine.
Most people jabber day-in and day-out
concerning subjects of which there's nothing much
to talk about.
The young ones think they will live forever,
the older ones are afraid of the whenever.
Ah, the loss of this bit of consciousness,
only fifty years later they won't be found amiss.
The euphemism "she passed away,"
is the telltale of their haunting dismay.
Even believers are troubled quite a bit,
they too are afraid of talking about it.

We are not troubled by things,
but by the opinion which we have of things.
Epictetus

Grudges

Oh, the memory wasted holding a grudge,
the warping of minds holding onto such sludge.
Should an insult, an injury come your way,
it's best to shrug it off,
and tell the offender someplace else to bray.
Suppose the "culprit" had a point?
Then it's up to you to find out
where you were out of joint.
And if the insult was out of touch
it isn't worth holding a grudge.

Hatred is a settled anger.
Marcus Tullius

Betelgeuse,

in the constellation Orion, the Hunter,
is the brightest star in the sky.
It is a red super giant,
at the top left, where it holds sway.
Arabs named it in earlier days.
If it replaced the sun,
it would reach out Jupiter's way.
About six hundred lightyears afar,
as a supernova it will explode some day.
In a million years it may,
or has already three hundred years ago.
But since the fastest means of travel, light,
is so slow,
it will take another three hundred years,
for our descendants to see it
flaring brightly in the nighttime sky.

Nothing is so firmly believed as what we least know.
Michel de Montaigne

Cacophony

I wonder, I wonder,
and am doubtful as hell,
that our electronic connections are doing us well.
Whoever wishes to add his or her voice
to the growing caterwauling of choice,
is contributing to an ever increasing noise.
While some of the noise is valid, alright,
much is vapid, inconsequential stuff,
gone in a minute, at worst in a huff.
And how to filter out terrorists' exhortations,
the sordid messages of the riffraff.
I can only hope we gain a handle on it,
that somehow we learn for greater profit.
I know, I know, worldwide people do connect,
but there is this cacophony of too many voices
making coherence difficult, I suspect.

Wise men talk because they have something to say;
fools, because they have to say something.
Plato

Friends 1

Now, that I almost took my leave,
my assorted friends, at home and abroad,
– about a dozen or so –
reacted quite differently,
some solicitously, some took a reprieve.
Casual friends came from the bushes,
others, closer, became quite intense.
Some must have had difficulties
dealing with my almost-demise.
One still hoped to save my soul,
so utterly hopeless is this goal.
Most of us have this problem
dealing with death.
When we are faced with it in others,
it drives home the point
that we quite possibly will be next.

It is better to be hated for what you are
than to be loved for something you are not.
Andre Gide

More Thoughts

What I like to do, too,
pardon, if I may,
is to stir up
the run-of-the-mill thoughts
of the run-of-the-mill day.
To entertain something different,
thoughts out of the way.
Sincerely, I hope, I succeed here and there.
If not, it's my fault,
my thoughts were elsewhere.

Our most important thoughts are those
that contradict our emotions.
Paul Valery

Literal

I've tried to write fiction,
but hard as I might,
nothing was worth reading.
I'm just too literal a guy.

It takes less time to do a thing right,
than it does to explain why you did it wrong.
Henry Wadsworth Longfellow

I disproved you, Henry.
H.W.

Namib

We once passed through this desert the oldest in the
world.
Our young guide, Kobus Pienaar, grown up on a
farm,
told of his grandfather's right
to shoot a trespassing Bushman on sight.
Yet, he himself, with a Bushman as guide,
had roamed the veldt
to take in the lore his guide's country held.
There came a day when the three of us stopped
at a massive sandstone outcrop
in the middle of nowhere
for our midday repast.
When done I clambered up the broken rocks,
a bronze plaque suddenly made me stop.
Securely fastened,
it wasn't large, held just a name and dates,
and a small rock bowl next to it
held the person's remains,

the ashes the wind had not yet blown across the
land.
What a marvelous place to find one's last rest.
The view, magnificent it was,
a memorial extraordinary,
his or her soulmate's bequest.

However grades the course of history,
there must always be the day, even an hour or minute,
when some significant action is performed for the first or last
time.
Peter Quennell

Incendiary Bombs

In World War II when Mainz was bombed,
my parents' house, two miles distant across the Rhine,
was also hit by five incendiary bombs.
Some were duds, others just smoldered.
Family adults choked them with sand.
I was just six, but I saw the city's conflagration
across the river, of what was to be left of Mainz.
Mainz, where Johannes Gensfleisch Gutenberg,
about 1439, invented the movable printing type,
whose mass production made the world literate.
More people learned to read,
if only to read the Bible in German,
which made the Lutheran Revolution possible.
Never again was the world the same!
Now, seven hundred years later
the computer, the mobile phone
– in a similar vein –
what will they be able to claim?

Satire is focused bitterness.
Leo Rosten

68

Choices

Oh, the choices we make
in jobs and mates,
some for good, others for bad.
Then, there are the littler ones,
no, not to have kids,
the wedding dress, what car to buy,
where to travel, what friends to find,
never ending choices to make,
many to enjoy, some to regret.
And after the years there comes the time
when choices are made for you,
which weren't your aim.
So, what is a choice called that's made for you?
A decision out of the blue.
What comes to mind is the whispering voice:
What fate is due you?
When you have no other choice.

Life is not a spectacle or a feast;
it is a predicament.
George Santayana

Do It Now

I'm telling my friends,
most are getting up, too, in years:
"Whatever your desire,
do it now, do not wait,
or in latter years you may shed sorrowful tears.
For your long-term memory will take you back
to what all you experienced,
while you traveled, met people,
on your enjoyable life's trek.
The stories you can tell
will brighten your time,
the ones you have left
till the sound of the chime."

A ship in harbor is safe,
but that is not what ships are built for.
William Shedd

Alone

We've found a new pastime,
well, it isn't that new,
or should I rather call it "concern" to give it its
due?
We spend billions of dollars, euros and such
to build great observatories, send rovers to Mars
and probes to the planets,
try to find planets around other stars.
Whenever some observations are chemically rife,
there's this ballyhoo for the possibility of life.
But none of the many implied planetary systems
around other stars looks conducive for life to
arrive.
On even the right kind of planet in the Goldilock
Zone,
it would take a heck of a lot more
for life to crawl from its oceans ashore,
and even more for intelligence to score.

While I do not exclude that one day we may find
somewhere out there,
some civilization other than our own,
we ought to realize that except for some amoebae,
we are most likely alone.

If you have built castles in the air, your work need not be lost;
that is where they should be.
Now, put the foundation under them.
Henry David Thoreau

Apollo 13

I once had the honor to dine with Jim Lovell,
the captain of Apollo 13,
his wife and some other folks,
at his fancy French restaurant north of the
Windy City.
Like the other astronauts I met,
he was a man I had respected sight unseen.
Irreverent as I am, I couldn't keep myself in check,
and told him teasingly:
That I thought Tom Hanks
had done a better job bringing Apollo 13 back.
But there's some truth to this story,
believe it or not,
for NASA had considered Apollo 13 a failed shot.
Only after its movie's success,
and the crew, Lovell, Haise, and Swigert
were received by the president,
did NASA relent,
and realized that the endurance and bravery

of the crew, with help from the ground,
turned failure into success
as, in the first place, it should have been found.

Being on a tightrope is living;
everything else is waiting.
Karl Wallenda

Meniere's Syndrome

For eight months I've dealt with Meniere's,
which comes in different severity, it appears.
Of course, my version couldn't be worse,
when the body purges itself
and the world violently turns.
When one moves through the house on hands and
knees,
or along furniture and walls,
when the world's topsy-turvey
made by this disease.
Sometimes the attacks are mild, as they come,
but still, they disorient, make sleepy,
for hours sick to the stomach, and then some.

The years, as they come, bring many agreeable things with
them; as they go, they take many away.
Horace

Proactive

We all need to be this to some extent,
but most folks let things happen, are content.
It is a matter of how much we care
that some of us reach out, are more aware,
make things come to be
from which others beware,
or just don't give a hoot,
much less, even care.
Proactive people make things come to pass,
most others would even consider a bother to ask,
and rather shy away from such bothersome tasks.

Emotions have taught mankind to reason.
Luc de Clapiers de Vauvenargues

Regression

We are familiar with the tantrums
of a child's regression,
but shocked when we experience it in an adult.
When some people, under stress,
their worth being questioned,
revert to the child, long since left behind,
but whose hurt is kept slumbering
until triggered, springs to mind.
Then awareness of reality is lost in a blink,
with social customs, friendship, and love
put into question, put on the brink.
The adult, thus impaired,
loses awareness of what he or she has done.
Those affected by the outburst are left
trying to understand and forgive if they can.

Deep experience is never peaceful.
William James

Existence

When I confront friends with the statement
that a rock does not exist
until it has been described and named,
they think I am nuts, maybe even deranged.
Narrowly focused on the physical existence of the rock,
they fail to understand the power of language,
without which our world could be a void,
mentally blocked.
Any subject, physical or mental, real and alive,
is unknown to a language
until it is named, understood, described,
incorporated into a culture's life.
This is to say our world, all we describe,
is a construct.
Even the scientific method,
our pantheons of gods, are existing only
for as long as we believe in these, our constructs,
until such time we leave them behind.

Language structures reality and reality structures language.
Benjamin L. Whorf

Miracles

Some people believe that miracles happen.
I don't, which is why they may not happen to me.
Content I am with the inexplicable.
A miracle it mustn't be,
a coincidence then?

Everyone takes the limits of his own vision
for the limits of the world.
Arthur Schopenhauer

Variations

Remember, friend, as you leaf through this book,
there is no consistency of themes.
Whatever comes to mind of the world,
is what I put down, usually fact,
sometimes a dream.
Do not forget what I claimed in "Contemplations,"
I'm a friend of Montaigne.

Every writer is a narcissist.
This does not mean that he is vain;
it only means that he is hopelessly self-absorbed.
Leo Rosten

Encounter

Back in fifty-six, on the Libyan plain,
we pitched our tent for a night to remain.
Later, we heard some noise not too far,
sleep became restless, closer it came,
then some bells were heard tingling.
A shepherd with his flock was all it was.
To our breakfast,
tea, scrambled eggs, fried pastorma, some bread,
he ambled over to join.
My companion, speaking Arabic, had invited him in.
The man accepted tea, eggs and bread,
after my buddy had tasted them first.
The pastorma, lean beef coated in paprika and salt,
unknown to him, he did not taste,
for it might have been pork,
which, being Muslim, he couldn't have faced.
He thanked us and returned to his nearby flock.
A human encounter we had had.

To him who is in fear everything rustles.
Sophocles

Fear of Flying

Only too familiar with it
I became when business required me to fly.
During the first year I needed a sedative
in order to get by.
Then, after the crash landing at Toronto Airport,
I decided to tackle this fear.
Thereafter, when the engines revved up,
when the aircraft sped up in the air,
my focus was not on my fear that much
but on pride of my species
who unleashed such power
to make flight across the world possible,
an accomplishment conquering fear.

Anyone can hold the helm when the sea is calm.
Publius Syrus

Lightning

On our first wildlife safari in eighty-five,
on the Masai Mara plain, we were, I and my wife,
with our driver and his native Kenyan company
owner
on an evening drive.
While there was still light,
we told our Kenyan companions that,
over there, on the hills bordering the Mara,
in "Out of Africa," Robert Redford died.
They knew enough, just smiled.
But then, night fell, and a thunderstorm rose,
to its lightning our two companions were ill
disposed.
I explained, if you count from the moment
lightning flares,
21, 22, 23, 24, and so on,
until the thunder crack reaches your ear,
you multiply the four numbers by 333
meters per second, that fast the sound travels here,

which tells you that the bolt hit 1,332 meters away,
not far enough, but in the car being okay.
This counting intrigued the owner very much,
"Why do you count 21, 22, 23, 24, and such?
He wrote this all down with my explanation,
also counting 1, 2, 3, 4 being faster,
would bring the lightning strike much closer.
There was also the Yukon killer mosquito joke,
our driver was unable to comprehend.
Repeating it slowly to our owner-friend,
who patiently translated it into Suaheli,
our driver, too, was able to understand.
Our searchlight's beam also found plenty of game,
like a huge giraffe standing stock-still
in a grove of trees, seemingly asleep.
It was the most congenial game drive
my wife and I have ever been on.

There is no safety in numbers,
or in anything else.
James Thurber

84

Ballooning

One morning, still dark it was in Kenya's west,
we rose, cutting short our night's rest,
for a balloon ride across the Masai Mara's
expanse.
The burners shone brightly at the rise of the sun,
when the five big balloons rose skyward
on our adventurous run.
Chase vehicle tracks we saw crossing the land,
long-necked giraffes and some elephants.
We rose high in the sky, then again dipped low,
almost touching the earth then rising anew.
Once we descended into the Mara River's ravine,
chasing a herd of hippos, a splashy scene.
At last we touched down to a breakfast, grand,
prepared on a balloon's burner
which had taken us aloft across this marvelous
land.
Then, we departed the Mara in a DC3,
its building dating back to nineteen-forty-six,

almost forty years old but in good shape.
The solid old bird was so slow to rise
that my wife was afraid we'd chop off the heads
of some giraffes, which, at the end of the runway,
browsed.

I am a part of all that I have seen.
Alfred Lord Tennyson

Navigation

Did you ever wonder
why so many stars, even constellations, have
Arabic names,
those who are interested in such obscure aims?
Well, Arab culture sprang up in desert realms,
and traveling during the heat of the day
was, while possible, not the most favorite
with a dromedary's sway.
Thus the cool of the night reduced this plight,
yet raised the problem of how to navigate, one
might.
Many a star or constellation is standing out
bright,
helping to find one's way by night.
Of course, all constellations and stars have Arabic
names.
The constellation Orion, The Giant (or Hunter),
like Betelgeuse, in Orion, Armpit of the Central
One.

Rigel, the Foot of the Giant, and Vega, The
Falling Eagle.
Then there's Deneb, The Tail of The Hen.
Thus, the desert Arabs' need to travel and navigate
by night,
provided us with names we still use today.
Never forget that other Arabic terms, lo,
we happily use today, like "sugar" and "alcohol."
And the star cluster we call the Pleiades,
after the seven daughters of the Greek mythological
Titan, Atlas,
forced by Zeus to carry the weight of the heavens
as his plight,
the Japanese call Subaru, "to unite."

Not all who wander are lost.
J.R.R. Tolkien

Falling Asleep

A few weeks ago, with a doctor's PA, I got in a spat,
when she labeled my occasional sleeplessness
clinically chronic, and that was that!
I did not feel this way at all,
for, except when the day's events did cause
aggravation,
or a lively discussion with friends
kept my mind churning, on the ball.
Most nights I am able to enter precious asleep
within an hour's time, for the night to keep.
Sometimes I sense myself slipping away,
but most often I'm suddenly gone for the day.
But what I fallaciously call a "poetic night," is,
when I fall into the grip of a power I cannot control,
forcing me to express my mind, sometimes my soul.
When new ideas for another poem
spring up during the incessant roam.
When in a half-conscious state
fragments of thought search for a better word,

89

bouncing between neurons and synapses, to better
create.
Like now, it may continue through the night,
till the early morning hours, it might,
only a couple of hours to subside at the break of light.
Had I waited for the coming day
to write down my thoughts of the night,
they might well be gone in bright light
with external influences, distractions,
keeping at bay what I had wanted to write.

Long years must pass before the truths
we have made for ourselves become our very flesh.
Paul Valery

Touch

When the situation calls for it,
when it is right,
I love to touch a woman or man,
and love to be touched in the right way, the right
kind.
It expresses a sentiment:
"I care for you,"
it crosses a boundary, brings us closer, so true.
A welcome and departing touch
can be tentative or hearty,
whether with a woman or man.
With a man it's often boisterous,
with a woman it can be both,
most often is of the tentative form,
where barely the cheeks meet, not a firestorm.
When I did yoga years in the past,
I recall a participant
who threw herself into a hearty embrace
all done with the utmost grace,

never implying something base.
Ah, to touch a woman, soft and warm,
is like Heaven on Earth,
if well performed.

In love, as in war, a fortress that parleys is half taken.
Margaret of Valois

Orchids

On the coffee table an orchid is gracing my room.
For three months now it stands in full bloom,
and still has more time, I do assume.
A joy it is to admire, to behold.
Known as an epiphyte growing on tropical trees,
it provides its own food, is not a parasite.
Twenty thousand species make it the largest
family
of flowering plants,
found throughout the world, on every land,
in meadows and forests, some small, some grand.
Flowers, angiosperms, arose about 160 million
years ago,
bringing color to the world,
in competition with dinosaurs' feathers,
as far as we know.

Not what we have, but what we enjoy,
constitutes our abundance.
Epicurus

Why?

Curious children ask questions an adult may not
know.
So, here are some answers to bestow:
Why is the sky blue on Earth,
when it is red on Mars?
It's the shorter wavelength of blue
scattered by air molecules, painting blue our sky,
while the oceans look blue because more
red, orange, and yellow are absorbed by water than
blue.
Thus when the sun's white light enters the water,
most that's returned is of blueish hue.
In mornings and evenings,
when sun and moon on the horizon are low,
the sun's and moon's rays must travel
through a denser atmosphere
with even more blue dispersed,
retaining the warmer colors,
the longer wave lengths of yellow and red.

Mars's sky isn't red but yellowish-brown.
Its dust, iron oxides, rusty,
absorbs the blue and scatters the red, giving it its
hue.
Yet, as we've found, sunrises and sunsets on Mars,
looking through thicker air and dust,
in contrast to Earth, are blue.

What is now proved was once only imagined.
Josh Billings

Left-side Problems

I have a conservative lady friend,
who isn't shy and at loose ends.
When once I told her what ails me most,
the sciaticas, hernia, meniscus, the lead foot and
heart,
all problems being on my left-hand side,
she blithely suggested:
"Herb, you need to lean a bit more to the right."

Half the work that is done in the world
is to make things appear what they are not.
E. R. Beadle

Encore, Love

Not until ten years ago, I'd say,
did I give the terms "Love," or "I love you," much
sway.
I thought them banal, overused,
facile, sometimes even abused.
I therefore shied from their easy application,
thinking to save them for appropriate occasions.
Yet what lurked beneath this rigid stance
was that I looked at Love askance.
Love, I thought, to be a secondary emotion,
second to engaged devotion.
Devotion to give things a go,
to get things done, to run the show.
I do not know what caused the change,
the insight of I fell so short.
Thus, what I missed decades before
was the serious lack of encore, encore.
And gradually, in the intervening years,

*I learned the meaning of this word,
and, lo, the shedding of some tears.*

Do not spoil what you have by desiring what you have not;
remember that what you now have
was once among the things you only hoped for.
Epicurus

98

Hatred

I don't recall a single case
where I felt apt, disposed to hate,
to ill will, loathing, enmity.
As I have written once before
one only hates what one perceives
as being stronger, better than oneself.
At root lies envy deeply buried,
unconsciously compelled.
Missed, it's a window on one's mental health,
or, milder, lacking awareness, common language
held.
Which is why I object when said:
"I hate this" when it calls instead,
for the softer "I don't care for it."
This, being more appropriate.

To acquire knowledge, one must study;
but to acquirer wisdom, one must observe.
Marilyn vos Savant

Dancing 1

Half a lifetime ago I decided
on the spur of the moment to quit;
dancing it was, and that was it.
I felt that I lacked the fluid grace
I loved to observe in others' dance,
was just too stiff to sing and prance.
Then came the day of some host's celebration,
at its outset, a friend asked my wife for a dance.
Not having danced for quite a few years,
she nevertheless gave it a chance.
With the festivities, lively, moving along
the friend's wife courageously and strong,
then asked me to respond.
I had sworn if ever I danced again,
this first dance would be with my wife.
Thus I declined the invitation.
I will never live this down for the rest of my life.

Principle traded for a faux pas.
Well, we were never again invited for a repast.

All women are flirts, but some are restrained by shyness,
and others by sense.
François de La Rochefoucauld

Social Graces

We've come a long way from ages old
when social graces were few but more bold.
Thus, the honorific "lady" was bestowed
only on women of such mold.
Today, in American parlance, it has become
a synonym for female-anyone.
It must be earned and, too, applied,
but all too often it's forgotten.
Emotion overturns what's to abide,
in table manners, gatherings,
when, like a kettle of cats,
they lose awareness, have no notion,
how to curb their excitation.
Let's finish what one has to say,
give him or her the courtesy
to finish what is on their mind.
Be patient, you will get your turn.

Let candles not at both ends burn.
And, last not least, before my thought goes a.w.o.l,
do close the lid on the host's toilet bowl!

Live on doubts; it becomes madness or stops entirely
as soon as we pass from doubt to certainty.
François de La Rochefoucauld

103

Fundamentalists

Given the chance they and their creationist spawn
would take us back to the Dark Ages,
we thought to have left through Enlightenment
behind,
before which myth and superstition ruled most of
mankind.
But they are still with us, insult to us all,
still held by faulty belief in thrall.
Hypercritical, they use the products of science
and it's offspring, technology, quite well,
but when it comes to these branches of science,
evolution, paleontology, anthropology, and dating,
they ignore and reject these, for they don't fit their
spell,
the darkness of mind under which they dwell.
Meeting such folk, I quell
any desire to address this citadel,
for it's no use, it only repels.

Instead I stay with their part of mind,
the rational kind, their God-given use,
or might even this be a fallacious ruse?

One can choose to go back toward safety
or forward toward growth.
Growth must be chosen again and again;
fear must be overcome again and again.
Abraham Maslow

For Annemarie

Mu-Lan, my Chinese Princess, you left,
and like with many a dear friend I've lost these
past years,
I feel bereft.
You had a full life, much wasn't kind,
but you walked through it well,
always kept up your mind.
I will miss our exchanges, our email pursuits,
and while we followed not like beliefs,
we respected each other, came never to grief.
I hope you found what you thought to find,
and live happily in peace,
freed now from the travails of humankind.

Love is an act of faith, and whoever is of little faith
is also of little love.
Erich Seligmann Fromm

The Hatchet

When my heart failed to work earlier this year,
a stimulant got me going again,
and a pacemaker then to steer,
all in all, my fifth surgery in five years.
I was so depressed like never before,
just wanted to die, invasive procedures no more.
These days, two months later, I feel better than I
have for a year.
I can do just about everything I do care.
My stamina's back, despite my ills,
my hemoglobin shortage diagnosed hemolytic
anemia,
when the body produces enough of the stuff,
but in an autoimmune reaction destroys too much.
For the coming half year I must every week
go for a blood test, which might make me weak.
They are pumping me dry with every tweak.
I swallow pills, which include prednisone, folic
acid, and iron galore,

I hope I won't be asked to add more.
Meniere's is still haunting me sometimes these
days.
The other week I had a spell
that lasted twenty-six hours, ah well.
I was able to sleep through most of this hell,
when the world turns topsy-turvy, like a carousel.
Walking, I sense a balance loss,
but I'll deal with this problem when the time's
right to cross,
which a one-hour balance test on the thirtieth of
March
will explore the issue in due course.
The only things I haven't done yet
are trying to walk a good mile, and taking Rikki
out for a walk.
But then she hasn't asked for it despite our
frequent talk.
I've lost a few pounds, despite eating well,
have a hankering for steak, I treat myself swell.
I host dinners for friends, cook my meals, but not
all.
I dine with them in places, am on the ball,

and am able to say too that I do have a ball.
The intellect works, thanks, very well.
What else can I tell?
Following the example of my friend, Montaigne,
I keep writing that which crosses my mind,
all without physical pain.
At this time I feel I've once more obtained control
of my life,
for how long it will last I can't contrive.
I take things day by day, but plan also ahead,
for without so doing I might drop dead.
Yet I can't shake the feeling
that all isn't rosy, rather black-brown,
and wonder when the next hatchet,
another ailment, comes chopping down?
In American parlance, I think, it's the other shoe.
Well, a hatchet is rather graphic,
but the shoe will also do.

Being defeated is often a temporary condition.
Giving up is what makes it permanent.
Marilyn vos Savant

Dregs

We cary the bad dregs of early childhood
forever throughout life.
Most are buried so terribly deep
that we can rarely, if ever, access this seep.
They remain part of our being,
for better or for worse,
whether we want them or not.
We can attempt to access and tame them,
but must also accept who we are
and make the best of what we've got.

The course of true anything does not run smooth.
Samuel Butler

Wondering

I sat on my deck, it's not yet mid-March.
Barely sixty degrees it is, still a bit harsh.
The first hummingbird, a few days ago,
did arrive on its long-distance flight, made it
through.
And I couldn't help wondering
for how many more years
I'll be able to enjoy inviting my friends in a jolly
atmosphere
for dinner by the setting sun,
followed by the rise of the Moon, full and round,
over the Bradshaws' rim.

There is nothing that makes its way more directly into the soul
than beauty.
Joseph Addison

Easter Eggs

When I was five, maybe six years old,
my father took me for a walk along a grassy road.
This was in nineteen-forty-two or -three.
There wasn't much traffic then, as today you see.
Into his pants-pocket, on the right,
he carried a batch of foil-wrapped chocolate Easter
eggs,
and, with a hole cut into the pocket's side,
he dropped them here and there,
so that I, ambling behind, just might,
lo-and behold, an Easter egg find.

Poets are people who can still see the world
through the eyes of children.
Alphonse Daudet

Me Too

The vernacular of "I" still strikes me oft wrong,
but since it's accepted in American language,
I too use it, whatever may come.
But I wanted to talk once more of my cat,
of a peculiar behavior she does have.
She has her own mind, is self-possessed.
I treat her kindly, for my buddy she is.
My friends think I spoil her when it's only respect,
for the being, partner she is, more need not be said.
But to come to the point, I'm sure she can't count.
However she knows the difference between a lot
and a few.
When the portion's too small, she goes to her dish,
to supplement the shortage as to her wish.
She loves her treats, she gets about ten first thing
in the morn',
then at lunchtime, for supper, and just before to
bed we turn,
a Betthupferl, as the German hotels call it,

put on the pillow for their guest to enjoy.
But, here goes, when I go to the kitchen for a little
snack,
she also appears, demanding her part.
If I don't follow her desire, she complains galore,
but if she gets just two morsels, she's content like
before.
I keep wondering how come she knows
that it's only a little snack for the two of us, both?

The meeting of two personalities is like the contact
of two chemical substances; if there is any reaction,
both are transformed.
Carl Gustav Jung

Hodgepodge

Reading Maslow's "Motivation and Personality,"
I realize what a hodgepodge I am
in my attempt to become human.
There are certainly aspects where I am ahead,
others linger, some are still bad,
imprisoned by what in childhood I learned
or what in later life induced me to yearn.
While I write this and similar things of myself,
I often feel looking over my shoulder,
my good friend, Michel de Montaigne.
Never before did I desire to underline text in a book,
or mark comments or questions in the margins,
but the itch does not leave me
reading Maslow's exhortations.
Maybe I need to relax my inhibition
not to feel "sacred" about a book's neat appearance
and it's revelations.

A work is perfectly finished only when nothing can be added
and nothing taken away.
Joseph Joubert

Irritation

What is one to think when a person is
irritated, fearful, of a hummingbird's pass,
the buzzing sound it is apt to make?
Isn't it that the bird's teensy brain
does know very well, much better than the human
one,
where it is in space so as not to bump into him?
Lurks something deeper here in the affected
human's brain,
the feeling of having one's composure impaired?
Is it just an automatic response to the buzz,
a deep-down fear, or what's the cause?

Science is what you know;
philosophy is what you don't know.
Bertrand Russell

Hate, Once More

Having given this subject another thought
I found that I can hate something after all.
As I've claimed earlier on, one can hate only
something, someone,
if this someone, something is stronger,
more powerful than oneself.
My smartphone, I barely use,
the intricacies of my computer,
the softwares' hidden secrets,
the newfangled electronics assault me, and abuse.
They are too powerful for me to cope.
I hate the power I do give them,
failing the will to understand,
give them their due.

Whatever you cannot understand, you cannot possess.
Johann Wolfgang von Goethe

Dancing 2

This is not really about dance,
but rather to sing, to hop, to prance.
To liberate, to release, and to set free
the animal dwelling in all of us,
to enjoy life with glee.
Thus I'm not talking of the stately, formal dance,
itself an expression of civilization's rules,
its ritual, traditional, dignified moves.
No, it calls on our natural drive
to express ourselves, to be alive.
This is why I quit dancing decades ago,
sensing the restraints from letting go.
An aspect of dancing I hadn't thought of before.

Our nature consists in motion; complete rest is death.
Marcel Achard

Fiction

I must come back to fiction
for Fiction rules the world.
Most people don't think of it as fiction
and take the Imagined as real.
What a world to live in,
a closeted mind,
prevented from exploring
beyond the narrow, the restricted, the small.
Curiosity confined.

Man cannot discover new oceans unless he has the courage
to lose sight of the shore.
Philip Chesterfield

Arithmetic vs Math

Most people don't know the difference
between these separate two.
Algebra and calculus are math.
Arithmetic is two plus two.

Thoughts like fleas leap from man to man,
but they don't bite everybody.
Stanislaw Jerzy Lec

Pithy

A longer poem has much to tell,
oft, but not every time.
I happen to like the shorter ones,
brief, terse, succinct,
sometimes full of glee.
Thus, pithy they may be.

I would never die for my beliefs
because I might be wrong.
Bertrand Russell

Captive

A captive of Prescott-town I am.
Sudden Meniere's vertigo keeps me tied down.
Upon its onset I can always drive home,
but to leave town, alone,
can no longer be done.
When the body must purge itself,
for six, twelve, twenty-four hours
my ability to properly function is gone.
Leave town I can, in the company of someone.
I can drive, I can ride,
as long as my companion will abide
by the caveat that I may need to get home quickly,
or to stop by the roadside.

It is in self-limitation that the master shows himself.
Johann Wolfgang von Goethe

My Little Carnivore,

---

is one of my endearments for my Rikki cat.
But when joining me for my siesta, between my
legs,
a fuzz-ball she becomes once her trampling stops.
At times, when I look at her beautiful face
I see the wildness, her still untamedness.
And were she able to have her way,
to hunt and ambush various prey,
a carnivore she becomes,
I respectfully say.

What delights us in visible beauty is the invisible.
Marie von Ebner-Eschenbach

123

Driven

I am to do what I must,
to acquire, to integrate in the time given,
myself, my being, to ever last,
before it's too late, before time has passed.
I sense the contradictions, yet the unity, too.
How will I be able to reconcile the two?
Strive I will, I know I am close,
yet there is still this distance,
somehow, somewhere, interposed.
I must do it myself, I'm at it alone,
a lifetime of folly must still be shed,
so much overblown, so deeply anchored
in the soul.

As you cannot do what you wish,
you should wish what you can do.
Terence

... and Yet, and Yet,

---

to just be, simply be,
at peace, having found equanimity,
not by setting a goal
but arising from the depth of the soul,
a Taoist distance, a rest in oneself,
letting go, yet being engaged in every sense.
Not an itch to scratch,
but with awareness high,
this would be the state I wish to achieve
before I depart, before I die.

Action: the last resource of those
who do not know how to dream.
Oscar Wilde

Enculturation

Ah, the encumbrances put upon us!
The rules, the don'ts, to be good, and thus.
The bunk we were taught, sublimated deep,
which keeps ruling us for better or worse.
Some is needed for culture to work,
but when I take sight of what all there lurks
through past decades, centuries murk,
the beating down of independent thought,
the loss of spontaneity,
the growth of the spirit never sought,
despairing I could, I know what I lost,
and not just myself also my life's escorts.

The authority of those who teach us is very often
a hindrance to those who wish to learn.
Marcus Tullius Cicero

Pursuit

These days sessions, vids, and print
provide a profusion of teachings on how
to improve one's life's ethereal sprint.
Surely, some hold plenty of bunk.
This is not to say that many such teachings
are helping people to get out of their funk
and find purpose in life so as not to flunk.
But I know of some who are at it for years
plumbing the impact of their childhoods
to better perceive reality.
Yet, after much time spent, still at times,
when they feel threatened
a defensive, sometimes defensive-aggressiveness,
surfaces and a child-like reaction
overrides all that supposedly is to be learned
but still has not been left behind.

Almost every man wastes part of his life
attempting to display qualities, which he does not possess.
Samuel Johnson

127

Weighing

I have a number of good friends,
more or less in the Teutonic,
not the more casual American sense.
We meet, we talk, and I've wondered why
these good people, female and male,
continue to converse with me without fail.
It can't be my accent, then, is it my pursuit
not to see things black and white,
even though I, at times, can make a point
starkly extreme, almost out of joint?
I can also be wrong, giving it another try,
but my image of the world
takes into account that there is much complexity
and uncertainty all too often unspelled.
Thus I observe, oft keep my mouth shut,
not that I can't also babble on a subject apt.
But the conclusion I must arrive at
is that I weigh issues before I decide.

The pure and simple truth is rarely pure and simple.
Oscar Wilde

Heavenly Messengers

Most are fragments from the solar system's dawn
still cruising in outer space,
not having been into planets drawn.
While they stay up they are called meteoroids.
Some are of stone, metals, some mixed,
but once they light up the sky,
burn up in the atmosphere,
to delight a small child,
meteors, they are defined.
Once they have crashed somewhere on land,
scientists call them meteorites,
usually characterized by ablations on their sides,
the black crust pitted, burned into them,
by their fiery entry through the atmosphere.
Amateurs thinking to have found such a one,
– and there are many in this throng –
are usually advised these are meteorwrongs.

Consistency is the last refuge of the unimaginative.
Oscar Wilde

Becoming

---

fully human, whole,
which Maslow, in his "Motivations" as self-
actualization,
Man's ultimate goal, so cogently extolls.
For existentialists an urgent call,
it is, has been, present for the writer,
a professed existentialist,
in his early years subconsciously,
in later life, with many a detour
– some may not believe so –
an ever growing haul.
There's so very much to be learned,
not just by the mind, but even more by the heart.

The heart has its reasons that reason knows nothing about.
Blaise Pascal

Outsider

Since my teenage years I have felt to be
something of an outsider,
not fitting, belonging to any assemblage or creed,
just being me.
Whatever the "me" entailed yet to be.
How often I said in earlier times
that I evolved in the nooks and crannies
of our civilization's washed-out Christian confines.
Some of this is certainly due,
enhanced by being an emigre, transplanted,
never anymore quite at home in my country of birth,
neither totally at ease in my newfound home,
although by now making up two thirds of my life's
syndrome.
Yet I do know, I certainly do,
that I belong to the world I believe in, even fit,
acquired through years of struggle,
by spirit and wit.

The secret of getting things done is to act.
Dante Alighieri

Ferment

There's a people spread across much of the globe,
who live by the Book, mostly that is.
Wherever they have been permitted to thrive,
inherent in their core belief's drive,
unique in their pursuit for the betterment of life,
their values, their continuing to strive.
They are the leavening, the ferment of cultures.
Because of being "better,"
rejection has always been rife.
Thus from Greco-Roman times to the present,
rejected, persecuted, and slaughtered,
they have paid their dues,
the Jews.

You shall judge a man by his foes as well as by his friends.
Joseph Conrad

Wrong Place, Wrong Time

Observing or watching encounters in Nature,
some in the raw, some on TV,
of the various creatures that can be,
I can't help thinking,
how happenstance oft is the fatal link
between escaping or being dead in a blink,
or whatever else a fatal situation may bring,
such as incidents of natural disasters and accidents.
Luck has a role for things to play out,
for creatures in the wild what's to come about.
Mankind has tried since ancient times
to gain control, as much as it might,
to change this "luck,"
its encounters with raw nature, illness, and blight,
to security in life in place of luck's fickle plight.
Yet as much as we try, Nature is mightier
and always will have the final word alright.

But in this world nothing can be said to be certain,
except death and taxes.
Benjamin Franklin

133

Thinking

Reading about it I've become aware
of why I enjoy silence over the constant blare
of so-called music in offices, stores,
departure lobbies, and more,
preventing those exposed day-in-and-day-out,
in addition to their tasks,
to give any deeper thought
even a few minutes time to sprout.
Such is also the chatter of folk
who respond ever instantly, intuitively,
from the depths of their "soul,"
or should it rather be said from their gut gone
a.w.o.l,
without ever giving time to reflect
on what may be wrong of what they just said,
had they only properly checked.

To truly listen to what's being said
is hellishly tiring which is why I truly dread
when people keep droning on, when instead
short bursts of information keep attention on track.

All our evil comes from our inability to be alone.
Jean de La Bruyere

. . . and to think.
H.W.

Existentialism

---

proposes that every human being born
into a world without Meaning faces the ultimate
task
of assuming responsibility for establishing an
ethical stance
as to what is supposed to be right or wrong.
More though, to prosper, even to survive,
is the task of procuring a personal purpose,
a purpose to provide sense for his or her life.
Thus, in my middle teens,
home did the simple thought, an insight, hit:
"To live life and to make the best of it."
To this day I recall the location where these
thoughts came to set.
At eighteen I exited the Lutheran Church,
never looking back to find security in a religious
belief,
for I do know with certainty – life is precarious –
that no true certainty can ever be achieved.

Thus, the basics of becoming an existentialist had been met.

I pursued these ideas and read, and read, until the question arose,

by what rules shall I live this life making the best of it?

And frame it I did, "To protect and further life but,

when called for also to terminate it, which I did, although with many detours and failures I submit."

So I've come full circle, back to Maslow's thought, that to become a whole human being,

of morality, creativity, spontaneity, acceptance, and purpose, of meaning and inner potential, this beyond individual differences, is the ultimate task.

To know that we know what we know,
and that we do not know what we do not know,
that is true knowledge.
Henry David Thoreau

Remembering

To remember or forget something at any age,
more so later on, when remembering fades,
there's a way beyond keeping notes,
to remember that which we promised
or want to take care of.
To it we diligently our mind must devote.
To commit ourselves to Want to Remember.
This is the only way
to keep alight our memory's ember,
even to fan the fading flame,
provided we make it our aim.
Better yet, do it right away when thinking of it,
and do not wait, do not delay.

The earliest desire of succeeding
is almost always a prognostic of success.
Atanislaus Leszczynski

Act of Will

Is it possible by act of will,
by attention and awareness,
to enact, to become, to simply be,
that which we decided to accomplish
- - by patience, consideration, and equanimity - -
by repetition to become second nature,
no, "first nature," engrained civility?
To interact at all times with everyone
as if our life depended on?

Action: The last resource of those who know
not how to dream.
Oscar Wilde

Ghosting

---

is, what I call, when in the midst of night
my racing thoughts on some subject,
in this case this poem, become a blight.
Then I rise, boot up the computer,
to put down, so as not to forget,
before the breaking dawn I might regret.
A hot cup of milk, with honey sweet,
a few paragraphs, even a chapter in a book to read;
then it is back to bed, and lo and behold,
in most cases I quickly fall to sleep,
the mind

Life is too important to be taken seriously.
Oscar Wilde

Humanism

One of its followers I am.
Of humanism, a system of thought,
not a religious belief, but a secular outlook,
based on the all-too-often human juggernaut.
It is by nature individualistic.
Can an adherent truly "belong" to such a group?
What is the group's coherence to give us hope?
All cultures we have grown
are based on some kind of faith, of belief.
Is it truly possible to grow a system of heart and
thought
into a culture to thrive without coming to grief?
Will its adherents have enough in common
to truly, truly give it a go?

For years, I have wondered if in the long run,
we, without reliance on supernatural, theistic
beliefs,
rather than rational approaches to human
concerns,
will find the means of creating a coherent commons
belonging to us all, to which we can belong.

To love someone deeply gives you strength.
Being loved by someone gives you courage.
Lao Tzu

Goals

Without goals, beware, you drift.
From your copious mind's ideas you must sift
– trust me, when you seriously check –
you'll find something which is going to fit,
to carry you on with purpose of mind,
if you structure this goal most clearly defined.
Then give it a run, do not lose sight,
and the world will turn luminous and bright.

We are what we think.
All that we are arises with our thoughts.
With our thoughts we make the world.
Buddha

Guns, Once More,

but only in a roundabout way.
Likely my analysis will even go astray.
There's a difference what Conservatives
in this country, the USA, call Liberals today.
I'd rather call them Progressives
for whom change is not a bugaboo
which prevents progress in the way Conservatives
do.
Progressives, by their very nature are less afraid of
change.
Conservatives, as their name implies,
want to conserve that which is dear to them,
but what other, open-to-change people,
also value oft in the depths of their hearts.
But, it is Conservatives who have the greater need
so that the have-nots, the "others,"
do not take from them this, their valued
conservative part.
So many keep on the lights at night,

more so than Progressives might,
obscuring more and more the beautiful starry sky.
And they need guns to protect their rights,
more so, I think, than Progressives might,
who are less prone to this deep-seated,
subconscious fear and fright.
In this complex process Conservatives are losing
sight
of what we together might consider right.

Let your enemies be disarmed by the gentleness of your
manner,
but at the same time let them feel the steadiness of your
resentment.
Philip Chesterfield

Spring Again

Once more there's this riot of flowering trees,
of crabapples, purple leaf plums, and rosebuds,
a profusion of colors and blooms,
in people's yards to nurture insects, bees.
Once more spring has sprung,
yes, another spring for my eighty-one years,
maybe two more yet, eighty-three,
or whatever I'll be given to see.
I take it a day, a week, a month at a time,
and for as long as it lasts
I'll compose and rhyme.

The less we know the more we suspect.
Henry Wheeler Shaw

Shortage of Love

Exploring my present and my past,
enhanced by my brush with death this January last,
I came to wonder why the word "love"
was almost taboo for me until about ten years ago at
most.
Through the decades before, in common parlance,
I found the word overused or misplaced at best.
There was this pop song coming to mind which said
"Love is only a second-hand emotion,"
yet, as I belatedly found out,
the word "Love" could have stood some more devotion.
Where then did this aversion come from?
What is it I did not learn early on?
My parents cared for me in their own way.
Both worked hard to get ahead every day.
There had been the War followed by years of
deprivation.
They had little time for love and attention.
I grew up in the presence of three hardscrabble women,
two grandmothers and mother herself.

There were no grandfathers only distant father
himself.
No sports to go to, no lessons to swim,
no music to appreciate, and what there was of free
time,
I was on my own.
There was negative reinforcement, they did not know
better.
Later, at school I rebelled at the latter,
with grades that got me expelled
having repeated the eighth grade twice.
Only then did I buckle down and read and read,
and put myself on the road which eventually led
me to where I've arrived today,
and from where I'm still trying to get ahead.
My formative years were spent
in my paternal grandmother's "Fire spitting dragon's"
care,
as I called it much later,
for she herself had had life's hardships share,
raising her son, my father, alone by knitting.
Nothing about this was ever talked about,
not a smidgeon, not a single hair.
There had also been the Hitler years

when boys were to be raised "tough as Krupp steel."
Love was a second-hand emotion,
as far as emotion, love, was given to feel.
Of course, these were also the times when men did not
express feeling such as love to their wives and tots.
Thus, I do not think I suffered from a surfeit of love
and learned to express it in my later years not
enough.
Times have passed, and I, we learned a lot,
or do we just become mellow as we age?
So, whatever it's worth in the years yet to come
it's giving love a go and then some.
And, last not least, to what it comes down
is to become aware how we grew up,
no accusations made against the folks who raised us,
for better or worse, not knowing better themselves,
and accept who we are and have become,
and not by past shortages being overwhelmed.
No whining this is, just fact as seen.

To live is to love; all reason is against it; instinct is for it.
Samuel Butler

Manliness

Guys do it generally standing up,
urinating that is, just open their flap.
Few are of the splatter aware
they create by the height difference
or just do not care.
From the splashing sound they unbeknownst
make,
one can easily assess their prostate's state,
or of a T.U.R.P. they are in need of late.
Why not reduce the splash and splatter,
open those flaps a little further,
and sit down, unmanly, to release the pressure.
And while at it do not forget,
"Do lift the seat, then put it and the lid back."
It makes for a more civilized performance,
I'd bet.

Being natural is simply a pose, the most irritating pose I know.
Oscar Wilde

Skewed

The human mind is a wondrous thing,
    often akilter, rarely balanced,
  whatever balanced is here to mean.
   We all know people, even friends,
 who are a bit odd sometimes, somewhere,
   and if we are honest, even we, ourselves,
  at times are somewhat kinky, I'd swear.
At least this is how it may to others appear.
    It is not that we talk insanity here,
 but there's simply no firm ground for reality,
        a reality of mind,
   of what we might call a normal kind.

No great genius has ever existed
without some touch of madness.
Socrates

Reality

As the eyes have a circumscribed oculus,
a narrow window onto the world,
it is the mind that creates the overall image
beyond the eyes' limited confines,
we, in years of experience, have learned to refine.
What we think as being reality,
at least in vision, is not just of the eye,
but in the "mind" of the beholder.
Thus, if our mind's eye creates reality
what else does our mind create we then label this
way,
a fool's paradise some of us diminish, some elate?

So convenient a thing is it to be a rational creature,
since it enables us to find or make a reason
for everything one has a mind to,
Benjamin Franklin

Redemption

for the evil that was done.
It could come from high up
if you believe in such-a-one.
But being downtrodden, here on this Earth,
it must come from the very self
through one's own actions.
Whether being an individual, a group, or a nation,
and no one can outrun
what was once done in one's name,
then as truth, but rather by misguided ignorance
beheld.
I think of my country of birth, far away,
and hope for it to find its way,
to become a beacon, not perfect, just great,
for the world to find what it so dearly needs.
The only redemption we can ever make
is by the very actions we take.

There will be vice as long as there are men.
Publius Cornelius Tacitus

I am Who I am

I did borrow it from somewhere, twelve years ago.
I do know where it came from, but so it may be.
Lately it has come again more to the fore
when I see people dealing
with their ancient incapacitating lore,
not knowing where they belong,
who they truly are, what they stand for.
Their struggle pains me,
with them not knowing who they are.
For myself I accept where I come from,
with all the pros and cons,
but I'm still checking whether I go astray here and
there.
I'm trying, I'm trying, to find the right way.
Others must find their own.
I am who I am.

Before everything else, getting ready is the secret of success.
Henry Ford

Heartfelt Wish

May you not, at the end of your life,
be troubled by what was not to be,
but rather have arrived at the point
where you accept yourself and others
like a flowing windblown saree.
To enter the nothingness clean without guilt
with only love attached to your hilt.

At the touch of love anyone becomes a poet.
Plato

Inverting

I cannot quit this silly game
inverting the beginning letters of a two-noun term.
It's fun to slip such an inversion
into the midst of a conversation by
causing the unsuspecting listener asking
"What do you mean?"
Some are discombobulated, others swiftly catch on
to such ludicrous compositions like
beaver eager, lumb duck, nixed muts, shice nots,
with worse to come.
And sometimes, just sometimes,
while no harm here is done,
it so happens that
the fit hits the shan.

Women when they marry buy a bat in the cag.
Michel de Montaigne

156

Cassandra

So many people walk through life
the source of their given names unknown.
A bank teller by name of Seneca,
when I asked if her parents were historians, she
gave me a frown.
I told her he was a Roman philosopher, a
statesman.
It was the first time she had been so shown.
There was Cassandra then,
at the Phoenix Barrow Institute, Dr. Fife's
secretary-RN.
I knew she was "antique," so I googled where
Cassandra was from,
as is my habit to learn what's still unknown.
Since then I have taken on
calling her my mythological Trojan Princess
of two-thousand-five-hundred years and then
some.
Cassandra made prophesies which came true,

but no one believed her, did her folks have no clue?
When last Cassandra took my vitals
I asked whether she would prophesy
that my Meniere's disease would be cured.
I surely would believe her gladly,
but she felt insecure, walked out on me, left me not
assured.
So much for modern Trojan Princesses
to keep a suffering vertigo patient injured.
Now I must see what modern medicine, if
anything, can do?

Imaginative, sanguine men will never recognize
that in negotiations the most dangerous moment of all
is when everything is moving according to their wishes.
Honore de Balzac

Hydration

---

is certainly important to maintain,
but the stock response bandied about
by doctors and nurses,
of eight times eight ounces of water per day,
sixty-four, by implication, they say,
has been repeated so often that
just about everybody believes it
without checking the facts.
And coffee and tea aren't diuretics per se,
they still provide water as research states.
Thus, it is time to look at this myth,
held like many others in the past,
and examine the factual reasons
when someone is weak and dizzy typecast.

The opposite of a correct statement is a false statement.
The opposite of a profound truth may well be
another profound truth.
Niels Bohr

Longing

If only I could hear once more
the haunting cry of loons
carried at dusk across a Canadian lake,
and see the sky painted
in the colors of the Aurora Borealis.
Maybe, just maybe, if I regain my health,
I could venture north for an encore,
for the longing to still.

To love oneself is the beginning of a lifelong romance
Oscar Wilde

Perseverance

Lately, as I keep roaming the past,
the present and future, too,
as is often my habit,
trying to enter the minds of people and creatures,
on how they dealt, deal, and will deal
with the contingencies they are being handed by
fate.
There are the people of Nine-Eleven,
hurtling to a certain end.
There are the Monarchs and Painted Ladies
who cross the seas and land,
again and again to propagate life
in evolution's continued strife.
There was my father, an illegitimate child,
his mother, alone, I am unaware
whether her parents and two brothers
provided some care.
Mother and son lived in a decrepit house
long since torn down, as was called for, of course.

Throughout my life not a word I heard
how the two through the years had fared.
The silence, to me, speaks more loudly of how
the two must have lived a dreary life
with little to do, not much to eat, and little to grow.
Comparing my life now at eighty-one,
all that I know, and all I have done,
then imagine a life more than one hundred years
ago,
how stunted it must have been,
what little they knew, what little they were able to
do.
Yet they rose from what meager life provided,
they did not complain, never derided,
and lo and behold in the years to come
they laid the foundation for me to become
that which I am and
for that which I still am working on.

Perhaps in time the so-called dark ages
will be thought of as including our own.
Georg Christoph Lichtenberg

Butterflies

Oh, about fifteen million years ago,
as DNA sequencing has shown,
a single moth, all night-time flyers then,
in the wonder of evolution
gave birth to the day-time butterfly clan.
And ever since, having spread out world-wide
to more than twenty thousand species of their kind
to delight flowers but,
with their beauty, our minds.
I have followed the flight of the Monarch butterfly,
traveling from the Mexican highlands
in three seasons north to Canadian shores,
then, in a dash, in one summer, heading south
again
to their mountain homes,
there to mate and repeat and repeat
to which they are born.
A cousin, the Painted Lady, at home in Moroc',
from there, in a single season,

crosses Spain, the Mediterranean to Scandinavia's
north,
only to suddenly disappear there once the weather
turns harsh.
Launching themselves into the upper sky,
aided by the wind ninety miles a day they fly,
to arrive tattered back in 'Moroc'
to find mates there, breed, lay eggs,
and in the wonder of metamorphosis,
go through their four stages from larvae,
pupae, the chrysalis, to become the adult.
This marvel of Nature,
more than any religious teachings, faiths, or cult,
makes me delight in the world,
makes me exult.

Men willingly believe what they wish.
Julius Caesar

The Human Touch

The other day, a Sunday it was,
I fell asleep three times, an hour each in the
morning,
trying to catch my breath between tasks,
sitting on a chair.
And when I checked my BP was less than fair.
So I drove myself to the local ER
to find out what was going on with my poor
stamina.
Well, my hemoglobin was way down in the dump,
no wonder, without enough oxygen, I had to
slump.
At first the RN had been a bit rough,
but after some chatting we hit it off.
And when I was discharged, she said:
"I need a bit of fresh air,"
and arm-in-arm she walked with me from the ER
out to my waiting car.

Amiably chatting we ambled there
but what I failed to do,
it only later occurred to me, was to tell her:
I love you!

Strange is our situation here upon earth.
Each of us comes for a short visit, not knowing why,
yet sometimes seeming to divine a purpose.
From the standpoint of daily life there is one thing we do know
that man is here for the sake of other men.
Albert Einstein

Compassion

Recently, at a dinner party,
two strict Lutheran theists, an agnostic,
and an atheist, got into a spat,
maybe it's a bit much if I call it that.
The atheist asked whether he would truly roast in hell
if he didn't believe what the bible tells.
And the theists confirmed that this is how it's spelled.
These days I prefer to stay out of such talk
since no solution can be found for any part.
But I couldn't keep myself from softly mentioning,
but the parties did not catch on to that,
that, if I imagined a creating entity
it would be genuinely compassionate
because for this we have the greatest need.

Those who can make you believe absurdities
can make you commit atrocities.
Voltaire

Striving vs. Luck

In the wake of youthful failures
I learned to go after that which I wanted,
to make every effort to fill my need.
And the times came when things fell into place
I pursued, desired, fancied, or craved.
While I gave Fortuna her limited due,
I attributed most of my successes
to my diligent pursuit on how things to do.
Only now, in my latter years, it is that I learned,
of how much the unknown, luck so often is hidden,
has likely played a deciding role.

Denn erstens kommt es anders, und zweitens als man denkt.
For, first things turn out differently, and, second, as one thinks
Hans Windolf

Sharing

I am part of the minds of mice and men,
of the fishes in the deep blue sea,
of reptiles, insects, birds, and such,
of all the creatures that crawl, and fly,
and the gamut of microbial fry.
Of the waters, the air, the rocks, the volcanoes,
even earthquakes, bye-and-bye,
all part of Earth's life, her vibrant being,
giving and taking as she may.

To imagine is everything, to know is nothing at all.
Anatole France

Tversky & Kahneman

---

in decades past,
defined human thinking as being
- slow and fast -
Mode Fast as intuitive, emotional,
experience-based,
Mode Slow, if given a chance,
is up to analytical tasks.
Yet, even Mode Slow, if not kept in check,
may still be tempted to confirm
the emotional, intuitive track.
When faced with an issue
few people can keep their mouths
for a moment shut,
but blurt out what they feel instead.
If they held their mind for a few minutes still,
what would then be produced,
by the luck of the draw,
might very well be less of swill.

Two things control men's nature, instinct and experience.
Blaise Pascal

Delusion

Deluded are you who hold as true
that which you believe
has been taught to you.
Everything, everything, we believe to be reality
– no exceptions –
in time sprang from the fertile mind of Man.
If you can't follow this rational argument,
check it yourself, delve into it,
and when you come out the other end,
still believing what cultures and religions deliver
has come from higher-up,
you are thoroughly deluded, my friend.
When then you are able to leave much of this
mumbo-jumbo behind,
you are free to create your very own ideas in your
mind.

All is in the hands of man. Therefore wash them often.
Stanislaw Jerzy Lec

Myth vs Reason

A question for you Ancients I have.
When you still gathered in painted caves,
Were you already aware at this time
that beyond food, sex, and shelter,
life needed to be given greater meaning
by myths and what became religion?
Did you realize already early on
that the human spirit
needs more than the basics of life
to go on?
And, as the restless human spirit goes,
in more recent times, reason questioned
myths' and religions' benefits and woes.
Reason without what we call heart, is a dangerous
sword;
it can lead us astray to a dangerous world.
No, reason and heart must be intertwined.

We live by our restless spirit, our soul, our mind.
This is why for decades, I do still
value two human qualities most:
Competence and good will.

The heart has its reasons that reason knows nothing of.
Blaise Pascal

Horizons

I had promised a young Lutheran friend,
that, for my horizons to expand,
I would one of her church's sermons attend.
Twice my willingness a Meniere's attack
prevented.
A third I would have interpreted as heavenly
intervention.
Well, today, I was up to the task,
but felt like a stranger in a strange land.
I thought I better understand
some of my cat's meows than what the pastor had
to present.
Well, when all was done and I talked with some
folks,
I told them: "You all look so normal."
But then it occurred to me that I,
from a different planet must have come.

Compassion is the basis of morality.
Arthur Schopenhauer

174

Regret

Something keeps nagging my restless mind.
What, when and if the time given,
all inconsequential things left behind,
there may surface from the mind's recesses,
until then quarantined,
a subject almost forgotten,
once very important for the ego, the self.
Long ago, then, it lost its import,
and the Self may ask:
"Why did I fall short?
Why did I carry this on
instead of calling it quits and abort?"
Let's hope it will not bring remorse,
but only regret, a little less worse.

To withdraw is not to run away, and to stay is no wise action,
when there's more reason to fear than to hope.
Miguel de Cervantes

Misery

Suspended between hope and despair
I spend my days, some worse, some fair.
Will the treatments I get,
those for Meniere's and hemolytic anemia,
the edema, the kidneys,
resolve my vertigo and poor stamina?
Not really depressed, suspended I am.
But for how much longer is this to go on,
my energy sapped, my falling asleep
whenever I can?
My friends tell me: "Oh, you look great!"
My response to this is:
"Yeah, the outside looks good,
but the inside is in a miserable state."

Our greatest foes, and whom we must chiefly combat,
are within.
Miguel de Cervantes

What's in a Name

Once more let me enter this vast domain
of how we define the world.
For without language the world remains
a nothingness, untamed.
A rock is not a rock
until it has been defined and named.
Other cultures than our Western one,
may have something else in mind,
the rock being a spirit, not materially confined.
As long as enough people accept something as fact
it is what it is, not merely abstract.
All humans created equal, the thought of free
speech?
A woman with two husbands, a man with four
wives?
There was nothing like it before the scientific
approach arrived.
Where to did the Greco-Roman gods disappear
when their power faded, a new god was revered?

The concept of nations and religions galore
the world will yet be seeing and saw before?
But people, oh people, please do not be blind.
All this has sprung from our fertile minds.

All that we are is the result of what we have thought.
The mind is everything.
What we think we become.
Buddha

Bootstrapping

What an odd metaphor this is!
Look up where it comes from if that's what it takes.
Yes, I did not take the regular route,
by getting properly schooled for a life to smoothly
pan out,
but messed up in my youth
when I was ignorant of what it was all about.
Yet, at some time I did catch on,
aggressively strove and buckled down
to get somewhere, wherever that was,
to succeed, be in control of my life,
and in the end, I claim, I did thrive.
But for the boots and the strapping I paid a price.
Well, we can't have everything,
there's always a sacrifice.

Man supposes that he directs his life and governs his actions,
when his existence is irretrievably under the control of destiny.
Johann Wolfgang von Goethe

179

Whimsy

These days, suspended between hope and despair,
or fatalism, as it were.
What's left of my afflicted body is a modicum of
mind,
mostly a still growing sense of humor of manifold
kind.
At times it is wry, at others dry.
I've always loved a good tease, a nice joke,
but lately, more than ever, I like to evoke
in my fellow men and women a smile, a grin.
From deep in my mind rises this play with
language,
whimsy it is which gives it a spin,
by which I can still elicit a smile,
even pulling my own leg,
for myself to enjoy and others akin.

Death never happens but once,
yet we feel it every moment of our lives.
Jean de la Bruyere

Absurd

Working with wood can be fun.
But when the dust gets up your nose,
you'd better watch out what you've done.
As a German saying goes:
Handling a wooden board,
cut twice, it may still be too short.

The way out of trouble is never as simple as the way in.
Edgar Watson Howe

Haiku

Silence so precious
annoyingly noise abounds
will man ever learn?

Never explain – your friends do not need it
and your enemies will not believe you anyway.
Elbert Hubbard

Congenital Defect

Yes, I do have one,
on my pelvis, the left.
It doesn't show, I look alright,
but oddly enough, whatever physical problems I
have,
they all manifest themselves,
on the side that's bereft.
A conservative lady-friend of mine
I once ventured this to explain,
was quick per her political domain,
and said without the slightest slight:
"Maybe you ought to lean a bit more to the right."

How is it that little children are so intelligent and men so
stupid?
It must be education that does it.
Alexandre Dumas

183

Droning

What keeps some people droning on?
Is their ego weak or, maybe, too strong?
Need they compensate or are they mental vultures
causing their audience to yawn?

Even things that are true can be proved.
Oscar Wilde

Body Language

No, not the one by which we tell the world
what we are up to or be deterred.
Rather, I'm referring here
to what my body tells me:
which is that I am on the way out.
Now, there's Stage 4 kidney disease, severe,
added to hemolytic anemia and the disease
Meniere.
And the prednisone steroid causing edema
and increasing pressure in the eyes,
both needing counteracting medications,
water pills and eye drops to be applied.
What other hatchet or shoe will yet drop?
When will these afflictions come to a stop?

Sometimes even to live is an act of courage.
Lucius Annaeus Seneca

Capsicum

We ought to praise the sailor Columbus
who thought, sailing west, to arrive in China,
instead acquainted us with America.
What all did we gain from this new-found land,
the plants, the vegetables,
especially capsicum to add hotness to our foods
and elevate our gustatory moods.
Others, today, we could not do without
like potatoes, tomatoes, and corn.
Then there are beans, peanuts,
sweet potatoes, cassavas, pineapples, papayas, and
such,
avocados, sunflowers, and the grains,
quinoa, chia, amaranth,
and, not to forget, the many squash.
And what would we do without cacao
to feed our addiction for chocolate now?
But let me return to the capsicum peppers,
my favorites of all time.

Many folks think the seeds provide the hotness,
when it's actually the placental material, the pith,
the ribs,
of which some are hot, some more sublime.
It is the capsaicin that makes me chime.

Part of the secret of success in life is to eat what you like
and let the food fight it out inside.
Mark Twain

Cohesion

A sense of belonging to a group or nation,
a deep-seated, unconscious cultural recognizance
of being, of wanting to be One.
A striving to deal with dichotomies,
compromising, setting up systems
for disagreements to overcome.
'Tis, to live a society as sane as possible,
as functional and beneficial for its members,
such as the Nordic countries, Germany and Japan.
The question now is:
Will the Nordic countries and Germany be able
to instill in their many newcomers this sense of
belonging,
integrate them, make them One?
Something the Japanese with their xenophobia,
their paucity of immigrants, have no need to be
done.

Who will succeed, who will prevail?
Not the societies of Britain and the USA,
presently riven by discord and antagonism,
unable to determine which direction to sway.

Perhaps in time the so-called dark ages will be thought
of as including our own.
Georg Christoph Lichtenberg

189

Be Good

Languages change,
become almost unintelligible through time.
But if we pay attention,
we can hear the changes we, ourselves, take part in
becoming a new given, a new paradigm.
Just the past few decades "you guys" lost its
gender,
and today can refer to a group of men,
or one entirely composed of women,
as well as one of mixed splendor.
Not too long ago we responded to
"How are you?"
with "I'm fine," or whatever would do.
Most often today you hear "I'm good,"
which incites me to challenge the responder
by asking "Which way you would?"
Almost all take it ethically,
which also isn't my drift,
when I tell people in parting

"You be good!"
Sometimes, someone looks at me askance,
wondering about my linguistic prance.
If still in doubt I then give them a cue
by saying "Just be good at what you do."

When in doubt, tell the truth.
Mark Twain

Thanksgiving

It was a few years ago,
on Thanksgiving Day,
when I thought to go for a treat.
I happened to meet a young neighbor
with his twelve-year-old daughter
walking down the street.
On the spur of the moment I asked:
"Do you have any plans for tonight?"
And since they didn't,
I invited them for dinner, alright.
Sitting down at the Palace I told the young girl:
"Whatever you like from the menu is yours."
And promptly she picked a T-bone steak,
the most expensive course.
Her father chided her that, when invited,
she wasn't to pick the most expensive dish.
To which she commented to her father that I had
told her
that anything on the menu was to be her wish.

Putting my five cents of wisdom in,
I supported her father in general terms.
Then the smart kid piped up, telling her dad:
"Now you can pick the kid's dish."
And that's what he gracefully had.

There is no disappointment so numbing
as someone no better than you achieving more.
Joseph Heller

Sanity 2

I have this psychology professor friend,
and while we talk about all kinds of subjects,
psychology is always close at hand.
No theme is sacred, well, almost so.
Thus one day I asked this man:
"how sane do you think I truly am?"
I continued, asking him to be honest and true,
not to coddle my ego beyond its due.
His response was:
"You are fairly sane."
Precociously, I had thought the same.
We shook hands on it,
this spurious claim.

To doubt everything or to believe everything are two equally
convenient solutions; both dispense with the necessity of
reflection.
Jules Henry Poincare

Bush Tits

They forage in flocks of up to forty,
yet many people here, out West,
are not even aware that these birds exist.
They flit through bushes, from tree to tree.
If you don't pay attention you will not see
the way they drift, spread across distances,
yet never failing to stay in touch in their spree.
They look like a river with air in between.
Pay attention, city dweller,
or you miss this small marvel,
dozens of little birds drifting through your
neighborhood,
without your having noticed them before,
even when they descend right before your eyes,
never afraid,
picking insects from the twigs onto which they
alight.

In summer they pair off to build a sock-like nest,
woven of spider silk, grass blades and such,
dangling from trees if you pay attention, watch.

If we could see the miracle of a single flower clearly,
our whole life would change.
Buddha

Victim

We learn to become victims in the social realm,
to which women are especially prone.
Added to this are personal experiences by either
sex
becoming deeply embedded in the victim's soul,
often encountered from early childhood on.
To access such hidden diminishment in later life
is frequently futile, is at best serious internal strife.
Worse it becomes when the victim embellishes
perceived truth,
even reveling in victimization,
without realizing how unworthy it is, how uncouth.

The best way to make your dreams come true is to wake up.
Paul Valery

Friends 2

I have a goodly dozen of local friends,
an equal number of the sexes,
to be exact, they are eight of each,
some closer, some more distant pals.
Four more, all males, I've known for many years,
live across the country, the world,
but we stay in touch by telephone calls.
In recent years dwindling became the case.
Half a dozen are gone,
no new ones took their place.
But at my age that's expected to happen,
the time will come when I, too, will go packing.

Men have to have friends even in hell.
Miguel de Cervantes

Anger

I know of a man who is angry,
angry at the world.
Because the world doesn't perform as he wishes,
the world must be wrong,
makes him quick in what he dismisses.
All too often his looks tell he's suspicious.
He knows quite a bit but it's not enough,
thinks he knows more, quickly gets into a huff,
causing him to raise his voice, an ominous sign,
and his facial, his anatomical gestures
leave no doubt what he rejects as being out of line.
His life does not seem to hold much joy
but what is one to expect
with such anger deployed?

Missionaries are going to reform the world
whether it wants to or not.
Oscar Wilde

Divination

A final time, allow me here to state,
that our world in its entirety,
created by our minds, is human-made!
Our species has worked generations-long
on a framework of how to perceive the world.
While there are differences among cultures,
the meaning of things small and large
by language is conferred.
As long as enough people adhere to meanings
assigned,
they are thought to be obvious, true, enshrined,
applying to the most simple beliefs
and including all religions seemingly divined.

Bottom is bottom, even if it is turned upside down.
Stanislaw Jerzy Lec

Faith

I do not have faith
in whatever there is,
but deal only with degrees of probability.
Nothing's secure, everything can change,
some in the blink of an eye, some through eternity.
Of low probability I see the existence of a deity,
which is why I can't call myself an atheist
because of that smidgen of probability
that there might, after all, a deity being manifest.
But the odds are so small,
they don't keep me in thrall. I just live day by day
until these days come to stall.
I've had a life rich and full,
with failures and successes
and when all is done, there will be left
some regrets and some sadness.

Courage is almost a contradiction in terms. It means a strong
desire to live taking the form of readiness to die.
Gilbert Keith Chesterton

Unitarian

I have this Unitarian-raised friend who,
with her husband, invited me to attend
the presentation at a Unitarian Church for a
woman's talk
of her Camino de Santiago de Compostela pilgrimage,
her intrepid five-hundred-mile walk.
Knowing of it there was nothing to lose
to learn a bit more,
and sparing myself my own body's abuse.
When it was over my friend did ask:
"What did you think of it?
not just referring to the talk."
I responded that there was too much peripheral stuff,
like hymn singing, rituals, and such.
Quickly she made the astute observation:
"You are beyond being a Unitarian."

Work out your own salvation. Do not depend on others.
Buddha

Awareness

Can we truly be fully aware
of something for which we have no name?
I grant, we can sense whatever it is,
but conscious control of perception must be our
aim.
And to share it with others a word we must frame.
Situational awareness is such a term.
While not entirely new, it only gained traction in
recent times.
In the late 1980s I named an idea,
"environmental awareness"
I called it to pursue and obey.
But "environmental" was too static a word,
so, when "situation awareness" appeared,
to it I from then on referred.
It is the conscious perception of elements
and events in time and space,
and the potential action to respond to them.

By 2000 I added the notion of "emotional
awareness,"
now "emphatic awareness,"
of sensing what is going on in one's own and other
minds,
a more difficult aspect of the situational kind.
Who of you reading these lines is yet able to define
their meaning and import for our time,
and apply the situational and emphatic awareness
of dealing with the world
through a more sensitive mind ?

I want to stay close to the edge as I can without going over.
Out on the edge you see all kinds of things you can't see from
the center.
Kurt Vonnegut

Lost

I've often claimed that I was never accosted
throughout my entire life.
And just as much that I never lost anything,
except for a thin mattress
a wind gust blew off from the upper deck
of a Lake Powell houseboat I had been sleeping
on.
But then it occurred to me
that I had lost another entity
I had known for sixty-seven years,
something much more precious:
In 2018, married to her for fifty-seven years – my
wife.

The mind cannot long act the role of the art.
François de La Rochefoucauld

Humor

The last thing, I guess, to which I'll acquiesce,
not reluctantly, and without protest, will be
my sense of humor, to reflect and to tease,
with the people about me,
the doctors and nurses,
the friends and family, as may be.
Humor, at root, covers the sadness of the world.
But for as long as I succeed
to light up a smile or bring a laugh to a face,
just for this very moment,
I brought joy apace.
What better way is there to leave this space?

Everything human is pathetic. The secret source of humor itself
is not joy but sorrow. There is no humor in heaven.
Mark Twain

Karpfenhof

the watercolor is called,
hanging there on a wall,
the mother of a long-gone girlfriend,
Margarete Tuberg Gundelach,
in 1953 on her canvas spread.
Decrepit this maintenance yard of the
Luxembourg Chateau
in Biebrich, my hometown, looked after the War.
Picturesque it nevertheless was.
Today it looks spiffy like never before.
To the left of the scene, torn down long ago,
stood another house even more decrepit and mean.
That's where father grew up
raised by his single mother by knitting.
Never did I hear a word how their lives evolved
in this place so unbefitting.

Still, when I first saw this picture
I made it mine, then a birthday gift to my father,
not to stir memories, glum,
but rather to show how far he had come.

There are some secrets which do not permit themselves
to be told.
Edgar Allan Poe

Maslow

Given the time, the mind, and the strength,
I will try achieving what Maslow recommends
in his pyramid of Motivation and Personality,
his path to self-actualization.
And should you not know what this entails,
look it up, dear reader, without fail.

Work out your own salvation.
Do not depend on others.
Buddha

Dream

In the midst of night I awoke confused,
and incongruent as dreams are,
heard myself twice shouting the name of an
unknown man
for whom I had no use.
Realizing I had had an all-too-vivid dream,
as congruent as they can be:
"I had been sitting at the edge of my mattress,
and, into the darkness had cried my
abandonment,
my loss, my loneliness."
But it was just a dream.

A man's worth has its season, like fruit.
François de La Rochefoucauld

Being One

Back, as far as I can think,
I wanted to be one with Everything.
To enter into the essence of all there is,
to comprehend how it works,
to understand how it feels,
to become one with the gamut of life
even its rocks immobile.
Not facile emotion I was looking for
but the empathy,
the acquisition of penetrating oneness,
to grow beyond the limited being of so much of life,
to become one, being one, with all there is,
as I had sensed it in passing at age seventeen,
standing at this Swedish quay,
singing into the wind and the sea.

There are only two mistakes one can make along the road
to truth; not going all the way, and not starting.
Buddha

Sighting

To what extent can we truly feel the pain,
the suffering of a fellow being?
Is it not usually at a distance perceived,
intellectualized, its true nature concealed?
Thus we only sight the pain
but rarely, if ever, engage the limbic system,
by which we feel, not merely see.
Just like two ships sighting each other passing
in a fog at sea.

It is only with the heart that one can see rightly;
what is essential is invisible to the eye.
Antoine de Saint-Exupery

Haunted

There was this friend of many years,
I had last taken to the E.R.
To Phoenix they flew him still that night
a blood clot in his left leg was his plight.
Confined he was there for two weeks long,
then transferred for rehabilitation to P.V.
By that time I was on
my long-before booked South American trip.
Checking my messages upon my return,
there were three in which I recognized his voice.
The last one, urgent, cried at me:
"Where the hell are you?"
During his travails he had forgotten
my own, final traveling spree.
Since then, every once in awhile,
I hear his voice, asking where I am.
He had died five days before my return!

I can't help being haunted
for not having been around,
when he seemed –
about which he didn't give a damn –
hell-bound.

Death does not concern us, because as long as we exist,
death is not here. And when it does come,
we no longer exist.
Epicurus

In Closing:

I Am Who I Am

When Moses descended the mountain
with the tablets he'd been handed,
he called up for the giver's name?
And a voice he supposedly heard from above, said
"I Am Who I Am."
I, too, make this claim
from where I have come
and to where's now my aim.

Not a whit, we defy augury; there's a special providence
in the fall of a sparrow. If it be now, 'tis not to come;
if it be not to come, it will be now;
if it be not now, yet it will come;
the readiness is all.
Hamlet, Act V, Scene II

Nothing worse could happen to one
than to be completely understood.
Carl Gustav Jung

Belonging

I am – born German.
At home in America,
yet at heart European.
By intellect Western Man.
Human by species.
Member of all life by evolution.
Part of the universe by chemistry.

People who know little are usually great talkers,
while men who know much say little.
Jean Jacques Rousseau

Beauty

What I will miss, when I'll be going,
will be the beauty of this Earth!
The harshness of her desert countries,
the richness of her vales,
her shores, her rivers and her lakes,
not to forget the life she bears.
So, what I've done throughout my life,
I journeyed far and wide,
took in her beauty where I found it,
across her seas and lands.
Her lakes and forests, up in Sweden,
which took me to Canadian shores;
from there to Caribbean isles
and to Galapagos, in time.
My true love, though, was Africa,
from where my ancestors bore forth,
the richness of her animal life,
which so intrigued me early on,
caused me to travel, when just twenty,

to Libya and Egypt's lore,
then to Morocco – and some more:
I stood on the plains of Serengeti, crossed
Ngorongoro,
saw Moon and Venus light reflect
from her Zambezi's waters,
saw them becoming Smoke-That-Thunders,
known better as Victoria Falls.
Three days I canoed the Zambezi, like I had done
before
in Minnesota and Ontario.
There was Namibia's rugged land,
the richness of the Okavango, the harshness of the
Kalahari,
and a Botswana, Zimbabwe and Zambia safari.
I swam the waters of Lake Toba,
sailed the lagoon of Bora Bora.
The verdant fields of my home country –
so beautiful – brought forth some tears;
and what delight it was to see
the west coast of America.
Sequoias reaching for the heavens,
eagles cartwheeling in the sky.

The Tetons, grand, like Jackson Hole,
and north of it, the Yellowstone.
Once, the Alaskan fjords were calling,
her lands, her glaciers, wild her lives.
The mountains of New Zealand's south,
magnificent, like Doubtful Sound.
And Turkey's southern shores I sailed,
to see the ruins the ancients left.
There were the hikes in Burgundy, Provence and
the Alsace,
and in the Alps, these old and civil lands,
in Tuscany and Umbria, America, and thus.
Now, in the autumn of my life,
I find experience more close-by,
in wonderful geology, so many eons old,
laid down so near my final home, the magnificent
Southwest.
And come the day, if I am lucky,
there'll be a wind right strong and fast
to blow my ashes to their final rest.

Where lies the final harbor, whence we unmoor no more?
Herman Melville, Moby Dick

Gaia

I am born of this planet,
I am part of it.
With its peace and its fury,
its starkness and beauty,
it is me, I am it.
I am part of Gaia's mountains,
her deserts and seas,
her forests and rivers,
and all life she bears.
I am her Mind,
who, aware, sees and feels.
Through fellow-sentients and me,
Gaia becomes conscious,
an alive entity.
We are her mind,
her spirit, her soul.

Let us hope that this Mind
will continue to grow,
to take in and cherish
that of which we are a part,
but which we don't own.

Anyone who keeps the ability to see beauty
never grows old.
Franz Kafka

Epitaph

When will it be?
The raven's croak,
a gust of wind to carry me,
home,
to wherever on this Earth
there's peace to find from this, my world
that slides away,
slips through my fingers day by day.
No longer pain of any kind,
again be one with
dust
which is
where I came from
before I grew,
developed mind.

Addendum

A Collection of Haiku Verses

The Haiku (or Hokku) was established in
Japan in the 9th Century.
It emphasizes a brief moment in time,
generally the natural world,
with a sudden enlightenment.
Japanese poets like Matsuo Basho and Yoga
Buson
composed their haiku in three lines with five
syllables each in the first and last,
and seven in the center line, a total of
seventeen, usually unrhymed syllables.
The haiku's appeal lies in its linguistic and
sensory economy.
Often an unexpected relationship between the
first two lines and the last is created.

Starry skies alight
once the birthright of every child
more to take away

From a mountain high
heavy tablets Moses heaved
below finding heat

Moonrise full and round
silv'ry light abounding
soundless tree tops sway

Surf pounds rocky shores
flecks of foam drift in the wind
brown pelicans soar

Supreme in their grace
cat claws can often disgrace
scratch marks left to face

Prickly their being
but oh the scent of their blooms
wilted too quickly

Roadrunner so fleet
springtime calling for a mate
raucousness is his

Silence so precious
annoyingly noise abounds
Will man ever learn

Asleep on my desk
her whiskers, ears, paws, twitching
my cat dream-hunting

Hippo pods galore
Zambezi moonlight glitters
hyenas laughing

Water pearls dripping
Spanish moss everywhere
Silent the forest

Water most precious
food is the next important
shelter reigns as third

At sausage tree camp
lion prides challenge the night
Wakeup roar by morn

Soggy high tundra
bushes and willows foot-high
Take care not to trip

Pyracantha blooms
insects sipping nectar hum
but beware its thorns

The peach tree bears fruit
the harvest this year looks good
birds have the last word

Deer walk through the yard
searching the dry scrub for food
Watch the coyote

Friends are so precious
civility we cherish
Do not break the strings

Sun scouring the land
monsoon clouds billowing high
May rains be gentle

Grunting through bushes
javelina search for food
In passing leave reek

Fifteen wooden steps
to make it into the house
Today one by one

Vertigo for hours
a prisoner of Meniere's
Will it ever end

Roman soldiers once
paid in part with salis, salt,
Salary it was

Lizard head bobbing
challenging neighbor nearby
Watch out for your tail

People united
linked in a cohesive whole
beware its discord

Flags waving today
July Fourth celebration
May it continue

The arctic melting
causing the oceans to rise
Global warming denied

Rugs most beautiful
hallmarks of the Muslim world
no creature images

Few have heard about
situation awareness
much for them to miss

Women are ladies
in contemporary talk
Honorific gone

Beautiful grasses
lacy seed stems arising
by grazers devoured

Convenient plastics
what would we do without them
Ocean destroyers

Pillows so cozy
rocking us gently to sleep
Many fights are won

Migrants cross the world
looking to improve their lives
stress lands they arrive

Civil behavior
societal lubricant
Such pity its loss

Gambling casinos
Indian reservations
Sweet native revenge

Chipmunks ever cute
scurrying hither and yon
A mess in the house

Loons' haunting calls are
wilderness personified
Ever less there is

Blustery the wind
sun-baked are bushes and land
fire threat everywhere

Hoarse cries in the sky
quail are pecking grain in grass
Beware the falcon

Grand Yosemite
sublime and majestic views
Mosquitos biting

Tarantula male
prowling for a mate in fall
Watch out for swift cars

Dolphins surf-riding
shadows in the dusky wave
Fun-loving like men

Condors soaring high
pan flutes sounding from below
their tunes so forlorn

Cruising the oceans
for years return to lay eggs,
No more turtle soup

Spiders have eight legs,
ants have six. No matter the
legs, both sting and bite

Fast as an arrow
cheetahs hunt the savanna
often robbed of prey

Wedding diamonds
thought precious like a marriage
Both carbonaceous

Exposure through years
to too much sun results in
melanoma tan

Galaxies plenty
each with stars in the billions
No intelligence

Smart and swift swimmers,
rapacious hunters they are,
Killer whale orcas

Vanes descend from clouds
rain never makes it to the ground
in fleecy virga

Miles north do they fly
then back to where they were born
Butterflies they are

Easy to hold an
opinion without data
Fallacious it is

It keeps on rumbling,
the nearby thunderstorm does.
May lightning not strike

A friend in dire need
Where the hell are you, he cried?
Traveling I was

Soothing the soft sound
the gentle patter of rain.
May there be no flood

The open window
admits a most pleasant breeze.
May rain not enter

Beach combing is fun
finding driftwood and nice shells
Today it's plastic

Quelea weavers
flocking in the millions strong
What's the worth of one

A covey of quail
little ones hatched twenty strong
What all could go wrong

Encompassing love
like a nearby nova rare
A consuming dare

Made in the USA
Middletown, DE
14 January 2021